Endorsements for *Silence is my Habitat*

With tender and unflinching prose, Jessica White elegantly illuminates the hidden rhythms of our world.
Fiona Murphy

Jessica White interrogates the world of deafness through the prism of her own life: not just the perceived division between disabled and nondisabled people but what deafness has delivered to her—the skills of observance and quietness, the relationships she has with the bush, with the sea and swimming, and with the corridors of universities and archives. She shows us how to truly see 'the triangular shadow of a flock of galahs, the scent of oleanders, the vibrations of cattle grids'. Through her travels through Germany, the United Kingdom, America and her own childhood landscapes in Australia, she reveals splendours that hearing people so often miss.
Kristina Olsson

Jessica White's reflections on deafness, on our entanglement with the ecosystems we live in, provide a new way for all of us to think about how we might take up space differently, how we might leave room for ourselves and others to live more gently. With heartbreaking tenderness and a thoughtful remove from the clutter of taken-for-granted life, White's insightful essays are an invitation to pause.
Jane Rawson

Silence is my Habitat

Jessica White

Jessica White is the author of the novels *A Curious Intimacy* and *Entitlement*, and a hybrid memoir about deafness, *Hearing Maud*, which won the 2020 Michael Crouch Award for a debut work of biography and was shortlisted for four national awards, including the Prime Minister's Literary Award for Nonfiction. Jessica has received funding from the Australia Research Council, Creative Australia, the Copyright Agency, Arts Queensland and CreateSA and has undertaken national and international residencies and fellowships. Jessica lives in Adelaide on Kaurna country, where she teaches and researches creative writing and literary studies.

Jessica White

Silence is my Habitat

Ecobiographical Essays

First published in Australia in 2025
by Upswell Publishing
Perth, Western Australia
upswellpublishing.com

Upswell operates in the city of Perth, on ancient country of the Whadjuk people of the Noongar nation who remain the spiritual and cultural custodians of this beautiful land. We acknowledge their continuing connection to country and express gratitude to elders past and present for their strength and creativity…Always was, always will be, Aboriginal land.

This book is copyright. Apart from any fair dealing for the purpose of private study, research, criticism or review, as permitted under the *Copyright Act 1968*, no part may be reproduced by any process without written permission. Enquiries should be made to the publisher.

Copyright © 2025 Jessica White

The moral right of the author has been asserted.

ISBN: 978-1-7637331-2-1

A catalogue record for this book is available from the National Library of Australia

Cover design by Chil3, Fremantle
Typeset in Foundry Origin by Lasertype
Printed by Lightning Source

Upswell Publishing is assisted by the State of Western Australia through its funding program for arts and culture.

Department of
Local Government, Sport and Cultural Industries

For my family
and Bruce

Contents

Author's Note	11
Grounding	13
We Were All Deaf During the Pandemic	25
Hostile Architecture	43
Intertwining	51
Swallows and Summers	69
The Breath Goes Now	85
Safety Jumps	103
Quintessence	117
On the Wing	127
Unseamed	143
Balancing	155
Notes	161
Acknowledgements	169

Author's Note

It is often customary to use upper case 'Deaf' to refer to those who use sign language and identify culturally with Deaf communities, and lower case 'deaf' to describe deafness as a medical condition. Kusters, O'Brien and De Meulder in *Innovations in Deaf Studies* challenge this late twentieth-century convention as it simplifies what is an increasingly complex set of deaf identities and language practices.[1] I use the term 'deaf' to describe myself. However, in keeping with the preferences of the deaf people I reference in the book, I sometimes use 'Deaf'.

Grounding

On Gamilaroi country, in the slopes and plains of north-west New South Wales, the mercury stretches into the high thirties in summer. The air is dry, the storms frequent and dramatic. As a child I would sit at the table on the back verandah, drawing or doing my homework. Through the large windows, I watched clouds boiling over hills, casting them in a dark blue light.

While my father ploughed the paddocks with his father and two brothers, their offspring – my brother, sister and me, and our six cousins – roamed the banks of the creek, building forts from the bent branches of ti-trees. Bright green nettles and grass grew on the banks from black, rich soil spewed from volcanoes millions of years ago. Winter rains sometimes filled the creek with icy water. My brother and I, squatting in our gumboots, built small dams upstream with mud, grass and twigs. We waited until the water grew level, then pulled the dam away to watch the creek gush forth. When the rain stopped and the creek subsided to a stream, we picked over rocks in the clear water, looking for those that were bright orange and stripey. The rocks, we were disappointed to find, lost their colour when they dried.

In spring the ti-trees flowered, clouds of pollen rising from the creek. The children were recruited to channel the sheep to the shed for shearing. My mother, grandmother and aunts brought tea and biscuits, but left them in the ute until the sheep were in the pens. To stop the sheep from peeling off in a breakaway, our fathers stationed us and their wives in the dry creek. We waved our hats and shouted. My nose streamed from dust and pollen. One aunt told me to tie my father's handkerchief across my face like a bandanna.

Afterwards, we sat on an old tractor tyre while the parents drank tea, and I ate my grandmother's hard sultana biscuits from a battered cake tin. My mother, seeing my red eyes, told me to go home, but I didn't want to leave my family. I stayed put and rubbed my eyes until they were sore.

The country where I grew up is called 'Bukka-Bri',[1] or 'place of many creeks' in Gamilaroi. The soft grass on the creek's banks, the speckled stones and the twisting water all lodged beneath my skin. So did my awareness that, before the land was fenced, many other feet were cooled by the stones and water.

*

In summer, the dogs liked sitting under the woodbine, a bush that smelled of lemons when it flowered, its long, leaved branches draping to the ground. My brother and I enjoyed the secrecy of its foliage and climbed in with the dogs and our toys. Eventually we excavated a hole beneath it, helped by the dogs, and pressed our sides against the earth to stay cool.

My mother said I was often rubbing my ears as a child because they were sore with infections. Perhaps my nails were rimmed with dirt from digging, and perhaps that is how a shred of bacteria, whose ancestors were the first forms of life on earth four billion years ago, entered my body one spring morning a few months before my fourth birthday. My mother, listening to my complaints about my aching neck, moved me from the bunk I shared with my brother and sister to the trampoline outside. The light stung my eyes and the breeze, still sharp with the remains of winter, hurt my skin.

My mother, who had lost a child not long before, was on high alert. She drove me to the local doctor in Gunnedah, who suspected meningitis. He told her to go to Tamworth Base Hospital immediately. There, the doctors performed a lumbar puncture, which confirmed that bacteria had travelled to the membranes around my brain and spinal cord, causing them to become inflamed. My parents were told I had bacterial meningitis, and I was doused with antibiotics.

My parents stayed with their sister-in-law's father in Tamworth. In the middle of the night, the hospital called them to say I'd had a respiratory arrest. They raced back. The antibiotics subdued the single-celled organism, and I lived.

*

The sources of bacterial meningitis can be hard to pinpoint, as it is caused by several different types of microorganisms, including *Streptococcus pneumoniae, Neisseria meningitidis, Haemophilus influenzae, Listeria monocytogenes* and *E. coli*. Pneumococcal meningitis, triggered by *Streptococcus pneumoniae*, is the most common and serious form of bacterial meningitis. It often causes neurological injury, ranging from deafness to brain damage. The bacteria *Neisseria meningitidis* causes meningococcal meningitis, which is contagious and can affect people living closely together, such as undergraduates in colleges or soldiers in barracks. Among children in developed countries, pneumococcal meningitis is associated with hearing loss in 14–32 per cent of cases. Meningococcal meningitis causes deafness in 4 per cent of cases. The bacteria, bacterial toxins and cytokines (inflammatory substances produced by the immune system) can damage the inner ear's hair cells, which translate vibrations into electrical signals that are then sent to the brain. Septicaemia, another possible consequence of bacterial meningitis, can also kill cells in the inner ear and the auditory nerve. These hair cells cannot regenerate, so the hearing loss – known as sensorineural hearing loss – is permanent.[2]

A few weeks after I came home from hospital, my parents suspected something wasn't right because I often didn't respond when they spoke to me. My father and I drove for a day from the inland to the coast to see a hearing specialist in Sydney. He confirmed that bacterial meningitis had left me with no hearing in my left ear and only half in my right, and possibly some scarring on my brain.

*

Deafness made me observant and quiet. I could not hear enough to join conversations, so my attention would wander to a honeyeater's beak digging into a nearby grevillea, the morning sun on my forearms, the thick scent of flowering oleanders, the triangular shadow of a flock of galahs flying overhead. On the long bus trips between school and home, I watched the sorghum burnishing as it ripened and kangaroos bounding through wheat stubble in the late afternoons. The bus shook as it rattled over cattle grids or veered into the corrugations on gravel roads, and the vibrations travelled up through my body.

I took this watchfulness with me as I grew older. I acquire information from people by using eye contact and scrutinising faces. Humans find it disconcerting to be stared at intently, but some animals, such as dogs, I can observe with ease, studying their expressive eyebrows to decode what they are feeling. On the farm I noticed, when rounding up sheep in the paddocks, that the flock needed to be forced through a gate. I watched the pigs wallowing in the wet mud at the piggery to cool their bristly skin. I knew that our half-feral ginger cat, Vincent, was in a mood when his tail swished from side to side, and that he was likely to bite me.

Watching how we slaughtered pigs and cows, and shot kangaroos, I realised that there was a hierarchy of animals. I asked myself where I fitted in this hierarchy, because I wasn't seen as fully human by people who laughed at me when I misheard what they were saying. I felt a kinship with animals and wondered if this was such a bad thing.

*

Until my mid-thirties, I depended on my family to survive in the hearing world. I relied on my brother, seventeen months younger than me, to explain what I was missing in conversations, and to interact with people on my behalf. My parents supported me financially when I was establishing myself as a writer and an academic. My sister was a safety net when I finished my doctorate and moved from London to Brisbane.

To be disabled is, more often than not, to be dependent on other humans, or at least more dependent than nondisabled people. This does not mean that others cannot depend on us. I am a ready audience for my brother's jokes and stories; I helped my sister care for her children when they were small; my mother was proud to have a writer in the family; my father, who loves quirkiness, has been gifted a life far more interesting than it might otherwise have been; my partner benefited from my financial support as he studied for his second undergraduate degree, and from my experience as an academic as he wrestled with his PhD.

Janice McLaughlin, a sociology professor in the United Kingdom, observes that care is often presented as something that only non-disabled families – and particularly nondisabled mothers – can do. She notes how families can change and challenge this, as well as other stereotypes of dependency and disability.[3] My brother and sister spoke on my behalf numerous times. As a politician-in-training, my sister spoke up for her community, while my brother raised awareness for LGBTQI+ employees at his work. Watching them, and drawing on my own experiences, I advocate for disabled people through my research and writing.

Interdependency – between the disabled person and their family, between the family and its culture, and between the disabled person and their culture – breaks down the divisions between private and public. Surely, then, the perceived division between disabled and nondisabled people and the wider world of their environment can also be dissolved.

*

Some of our dependency on the natural world is obvious: without plants, humans do not have the oxygen and sugar they need to stay alive. Without wood, clay and stones, we do not have shelter. The adult human body is between 50–70 per cent water, and approximately half of it is made up of bacteria.[4] Other dependencies are less noticeable, although researchers are bringing them to light. In the United States in 2006, *Pseudogymnoascus destructans*, a white fungus, began to grow on the noses of hibernating bats in winter, and decimated their populations. The bats' diet includes large quantities of insects, so in their absence, farmers increased their use of pesticides by an average of almost a third. This in turn affected infant mortality. Counties that housed the bats with the fungus revealed an infant death rate of 7.9 per cent higher (on average) than counties that had healthy bats.[5] The lives and fates of bats and small children are intertwined.

It seems to me, then, that if I am to write about a human life, I must inevitably write about nonhuman life. After all, as Deaf writer Fiona Murphy explains in her memoir, *The Shape of Sound*, 'how we understand the world is through our bodies and how we understand our bodies is through the world'.[6]

These ideas motivated and shaped the book I have been writing for more than half my life, an ecobiography of nineteenth-century botanist Georgiana Molloy (1805–1843). Molloy and her husband emigrated from England to Augusta in south-west Western Australia in 1829 and were among the first wadjelas (white people) to remain in the area. For twenty-three years I have been travelling to Wadandi Noongar boodja (the Noongar word for 'country'), trying to get a sense of how the light falls, the sounds of the creeks, oceans and birds, what the soil and blossoms smell like, and how the country changed Georgiana. For all this time I have been trying to write about her life in a way that gives weight to the richness of the species she encountered.

In 2016, courtesy of a postdoctoral fellowship, I could finally research the form I thought the book should take: ecobiography. Where a biography recounts a human life, an ecobiography shows how that life has been shaped by its ecosystems.

At the end of the fellowship, I planned to travel to Germany, Scotland and the United States on residencies to finish the book. But a series of events caused it to stall. Covid-19 interrupted the residencies in 2020, precipitating my return to Australia. A year later I uprooted myself and moved to Adelaide, on Kaurna country, for a new job. I had to learn to live without my partner, Bruce, who remained in Brisbane to work on his PhD. In 2023, I gained momentum on the book once more and travelled to Scotland on my long-delayed research trip, retracing Georgiana's steps as she toured the lochs and peninsulas west of Dunbartonshire in 1828.

I flew back into Sydney on the day after my mother's birthday and stayed with friends. When I ventured out for coffee, I called my mother to wish her a belated happy birthday. She had been ill for many years with a chronic lung infection and was on oxygen most of the time. When we Skyped while I was in Scotland, she had talked about euthanasia. She was waiting for it to become legal in New South Wales.

'How have you been?' I asked her, ambling alongside the raised wooden beds of the community vegetable garden near my friends' house.

'Not too good. I'm afraid this is the end.'

'Oh.' My throat swallowed all my sentences.

'I'm sorry, but I just can't do it anymore.'

I made another trip to Armidale, where my parents lived. Mum went onto a different kind of morphine, and rallied. I flew back home to Adelaide.

*

In October 2023, in our family group chat, we discussed when my brother, in America, would come back for Christmas. We figured it would be our last one as a family. My mother added, *Jess what about the book – I need it done to die in peace.*

The first draft will be done by Xmas eve. Stop harassing me about it, I replied.

My brother chimed in. *'I'm dying, you have to finish your book.' Your publisher couldn't hope for a better motivation. Poor Jess, I'll bring you coffees.*

My mother began to decline again. She called me at work to say, once more, that she couldn't go on. My brother moved his trip forward and my sister, who had finished cycling 200 kilometres on a fundraising venture, drove down from Brisbane.

In Armidale, we gathered around the television, happy to be together again, and drank champagne. 'Mum looks like she's ready to play a game of squash,' my father joked.

The euthanasia legislation in New South Wales passed, but it would still take until January before my mother could access the drugs. I could see she was struggling to make a decision. My sister and I had to return to our jobs. Accustomed to thinking that we had more time,

I figured that I would wrap things up at work and then return to Armidale to write the first draft of the book before Christmas.

In November, after a sudden, sharp decline – possibly from septicaemia – my mother died.

In the weeks following, I moved as though underwater, my body dragging with fatigue. I napped on the bed with my father's whippet, Olive. My partner stayed for six weeks, and when he was fed up with my family I booked a ticket for him from Brisbane to Armidale, instead of the other way around. It was the first time I'd ever made a mistake with booking flights.

I could not feel a great deal, not even much guilt that I hadn't finished the book. I had the fortune to be seeing a good psychologist, a pragmatic and humorous woman. Recognising that I was a workaholic, she recommended exercise and some work, by way of structure. I was secretly glad that I had permission to write; the long days were crushing in their formlessness.

I returned to the book, but its lack of movement frustrated me. I had not wanted to write it in a linear way but, numb and dazed, I could not think how else to structure it. The architecture of the book and all it contained – plants, insects, birds, settler-invaders, botanical connoisseurs, Wadandi Noongar custodians, ships and Wardian cases – all folded like an avalanche. I stood in the dust of my words, bewildered.

*

There are old Greek stories about Demeter, the goddess of the harvest, seeking her lost daughter Persephone, who had been abducted by

Hades and taken to the underworld. Demeter caused the whole world to go hungry in her desperation to find her daughter, until Zeus, via Hermes, fetched her back. These stories are chthonic, a term that comes from an Ancient Greek word *khthōn* meaning 'earth'. They relate to the underworld and to things that grow from the earth.

Where are the chthonic stories of daughters searching for their mothers in the afterlife? Of waiting for her to return to the human realm as if she had been away for a trip, suitcase in hand and a bright smile on her face? Where are the stories that prepare you for the incomprehension when you walk through the door of your family home and see her empty chair? Unable to find any, I needed to create my own template for managing my grief. I turned, as I have for most of my life, to writing.

To write an essay is to make an attempt, to test or try out one's responses to a subject, emotionally, intellectually and psychologically.[7] The word's etymology indicates that it comes from the Old French *assaier*, a variant of *essai*, meaning 'trial' and *essayer* meaning 'to try'. Perhaps this is why I turned to the form in the year following my mother's death. These essays are attempts to work out who I am in a world without her, and what kind of writer I am now that she is no longer my reader.

We Were All Deaf During the Pandemic

When Covid-19 began to jump borders in January 2020, I was on a writing fellowship at the Rachel Carson Center for Environment and Society in Munich. Germany's first few cases were sent to Schwabing Hospital, not far from where I lived and worked. I didn't think much of it, assuming that it would be contained.

As the severity of the virus became apparent, I reluctantly booked a flight back home. A Singaporean colleague at the Rachel Carson Center said the airports were closing and recommended that I return earlier. I moved my flight forward by a week and checked the Qantas website every day for updates. Too frightened to go outside in case I was infected and stranded in Germany, I arranged for a friend to drop off some food. I started to get cabin fever and Skyped Bruce in a panic. He offered some philosophical advice: everything is beyond our control, so there's no point in getting agitated. It kept me calm for a few more hours.

On the news I read that Dubai, where my flight stopped over, was closing its airport. I checked the dates on my ticket again – my flight departed at 10.30am and the airport was due to close at 12.00pm. Unwilling to call Qantas, because it is hard for me to hear on the phone, and because my brother had been on hold to them for four and half hours the previous week to get back to America from Australia, I contacted them via Twitter's messaging service. I didn't receive a reply.

Finally, I took a taxi to Munich Airport, which was eerily empty. On the departure board, I looked for my flight to locate the gate, and instead saw 'Cancelled'. The Emirates desk was abandoned.

I found a young man at a nearby desk and asked, 'Sprichst du Englisch?'

'Yes.'

'Do you know where the Emirates staff are?'

'Emirates is closed.'

'I can't get home,' I told him, more to speak my distress aloud than anything else. Although, as an adult, I can manage my disability without too much stress, in situations when I don't know what will happen or if I will hear, my anxiety soars. I knew I needed to control it and stay calm.

I found a seat and contacted Qantas via Twitter's messaging service again. A sales assistant replied that the cancellations were at Emirates' end and that I would get a refund or a voucher. I then texted my kind friend who had bought me the groceries, and she advised me to check into an airport hotel to work out what to do next.

In the bitter winter night, I waited for the airport bus to the hotel. In my fatigue and confusion, I stepped onto the bus heading in the opposite direction from the hotel, and had to stay on it until it looped back the other way.

The concierge at the hotel, when I explained that Qantas had cancelled my flight, was sympathetic.

'Perhaps try your consulate?' he suggested. He booked me into a room festooned with pink plastic flowers and a shag pile carpet.

With four walls around me and some quietness, I felt more secure. I connected my hearing aid to Bluetooth and contacted the Australian consulate in Germany. The call was redirected to Canberra. When it connected, the Australian woman spoke so quickly that I couldn't understand what she was saying.

'I'm sorry,' I interrupted her, 'but I'm deaf and I need you to speak more slowly.'

She cleared her throat. 'We're not offering government assistance with flights at this stage. You need to make your own way home. You should go back to the airline, regardless of how long it takes, and get them to sort it out.'

I sent a series of increasingly desperate messages via Twitter, but my Qantas contact only replied tersely that the borders were closing everywhere and flights were being cancelled.

My brother called me on WhatsApp and we went through flight options on the internet. Some needed a doctor's confirmation that I wasn't sick, but as I didn't speak German I didn't know how to arrange this. Eventually we found an exorbitant flight with Qatar Airlines, leaving the next morning and arriving in Sydney. I keyed in my credit card details.

By now it was 3am. Although I urgently needed sleep, I was fearful that I would not feel my vibrating alarm and miss the flight. I took a long shower, repacked my bag, ate a sandwich that I'd made the day before, and caught a taxi back to the airport.

While in the waiting area in the largely empty airport, passing the hours before we boarded, I wrote about my ordeal on Twitter. When I finally arrived back in Australia, I discovered that an academic in Wollongong who I'd never met had messaged me to ask how she could help.

Finally, we boarded. There were only six passengers on the plane. The air hostesses, with little to do, were attentive. They passed me a pamphlet on how to join their frequent flyer scheme. The skin between my fingers cracked from too much handwashing and stung when I poured sanitiser onto it.

*

I was desperate to get back to my partner in Brisbane, but didn't want to risk infecting him in case I had the virus. We discussed whether I should isolate in a hotel for the recommended fortnight, but I had taken leave without pay from my academic position to pursue the residencies in Germany, Scotland and America, and my finances were tight. My chest constricted at the thought of being penned up, circling the small perimeter of a room for exercise.

There was another option: my parents' holiday house on the northern New South Wales coast, which they had bought for winter stays because the sea breezes were better for my mother's lungs than the thin, cold air of the New England tablelands. We decided that I would isolate there and work out how to get to Brisbane later. I booked another flight from Sydney to the Gold Coast, and a taxi from the Gold Coast airport to the holiday house.

When I touched down in Sydney, I texted my family. Bruce, a man of minimal expression, replied with 'Hooray for that' and an emoticon. Later, he quietly relayed his relief when he had received my message.

Staff handed out masks as we stood in a long queue at Sydney Airport. I rely on reading a whole face for meaning, not just lips, so not only was I unable to figure out what people were saying, but half of my usual information for communicating was cut out. At the end of the queue, we had our temperatures checked and were gathered into groups so that a doctor could explain the rules regarding self-isolation. I told him that I was deaf and needed to lip-read. He couldn't remove his mask, so he took me aside and spoke to me loudly.

I moved on to Immigration. The woman behind the desk unleashed a torrent of words, and I put my hand up to stop her.

'I'm sorry, but I'm deaf, and I can't lip-read you with the mask on.'

She pulled her mask down.

When I finally reached the Gold Coast airport the next day, I pushed my suitcase past a line of hopeful taxi drivers.

'Do you need a ride?'

'No thank you, I've already prebooked a lift.'

'How much did you pay? We can do it for cheaper.'

I shook my head. I knew they needed work, but the logistics of declining the ride I had booked were beyond me in my deaf, jetlagged state.

In the taxi, straining to hear from the back seat, I listened to the driver suggest that the virus had come to Italy from China because of factory workers in the textile industry moving between the two countries. I wasn't sure if I heard the whole story, or if I should believe him.

Finally, we reached the holiday house in the potholed cul-de-sac. Another generous friend had shopped for me, let herself in, and arranged the groceries neatly on the kitchen bench. I nearly cried with relief.

The next day, the government forced all international travellers into mandatory hotel quarantine.

*

For the first week, unable to get out of bed, I slept. With a sore throat and a cold, I thought at first I had the virus – but without a car I couldn't attend a fever clinic. I phoned a local doctor, who recommended I monitor my symptoms. Over the next few days they subsided, and I realised they'd been a reaction to stress.

In the second week I dragged myself to the kitchen table to meet a deadline for an online workshop at the Rachel Carson Center. The centre had honoured our fellowships and was committed to supporting our research via online meetings. Between paragraphs I took in my limited view. I looked out to the neighbour's golden rain tree, yellow flowers falling over the fence. I saw a fruiting beehive ginger plant nestled in the long grass, the flower of red overlapping cones striking against its spiky leaves. Slowly, where I was became familiar: not so much the view from the table but a *pattern*, a way of being in this strange, quiet world. I had, after all, been in isolation for most of my life.

As it was hard and tiring to interact when I was young, I found it easier to absorb myself in books. Characters and places were more engaging than those I couldn't hear in real life. I forced myself to ignore my chronic longing for other people, even though it surrounded me like dry air waiting for the touch of rain. I worked all the time – writing, researching and thinking – to fill the empty hours.

Now, as I cooked, read books and pushed myself to meet my word count each day, I slotted back into the practice of managing my isolation. Since I was young, I have tried to focus not on yearning for what is sometimes out of reach (a hug, an easy face-to-face conversation, a laugh with friends), but rather on what I do have (time to read, write and rest). I curtailed my desire for Bruce across the border, which was closed. In any case, the bus had stopped running and we don't own a car.

At first I was surprised by how quickly I adapted to the situation. I soon realised that deafness had prepared me for surviving the pandemic.

*

Everyone jumped online: Skype, Zoom, GoToMeeting, Teams, FaceTime. At first it was fun: people loved dates with wine, fancy-dress office meetings and jokes about not wearing pants. Then they started to get a bit tired. They had to concentrate harder than usual to work out when to speak. Poor connections distorted the sound. Background noise invaded when people forgot to mute themselves. Articles appeared about Zoom fatigue, caused by an inability to access body language in a virtual space.

I confess to smirking as I read these. For me, every day is an online conversation, with or without a pandemic. Sentences are broken. Loud noises interfere. There's a lag as I try to decode what someone has said. I am permanently exhausted from the huge amount of processing my brain has to do to function in the world.

I, too, resented the Covid-19 sweep to online interaction. I was unable to understand my colleagues in Munich when we met via Zoom for our weekly workshops, and I had to pay for a captioner. I was cranky with my noisy family on Skype when they forgot I was deaf and spoke too fast and over the top of one another. Yet another part of me relished the tiredness that nondisabled people were experiencing in isolation. Without the pandemic, they would never understand what it's like to be deaf. Now there was a chance they would.

*

In the third week I was released from my confinement. I left my inside-out view, blinkered by the verandah doors, of the raintree, the ginger plant and the patch of overgrown lawn. I walked up a steep hill, passing driveways, garden beds, mailboxes.

Noisy roads and planes hurt my ears and make it hard to carry out a conversation. I strain to decode words against the roar of background noise, my heart rate rising with frustration and anxiety. Now, as I moved through the streets, my shoulders relaxed, because the cars were sporadic and I could walk on the tarmac without fear of being run over.

I passed a man bringing his wheelie bin in from the kerb. He veered away when he saw me and we both smiled, a little sheepish. I crossed a bridge over a clear creek where small stingrays swam. The creek was fringed by mangroves, their roots exposed by low tide. The rich, dank smell of the mud reached my nose. When I saw the sea, a dark line against the horizon, my body filled with light.

*

As a child I would wake early, staring at the slats of the bunk above me while I waited for my brother to rise out of sleep. Some sounds, like bird calls, I can hear well. Lying in my bed, I listened to the three-note call of a lousy jack, or apostle bird, in the apricot tree outside my window. It sounded like it was calling the three syllables of my name: *Jess – i – ca*. Most of the time, though, I rely on other senses to feel present in the world: a hot summer breeze breathing on my face; Dad's whippet's smooth flank, warm to touch from the sun as she dozes on the brick porch; the texture of smells in the garden from climbing roses and lemon verbena after rain.

*

As people came out of isolation, the world rushed at their senses, the way it has always rushed at mine.

On the beach, sand crusted my feet. The waves, still warm from summer, fizzed against my calves. Large black butterflies rode the breezes, dipping to the water to sip salt. I watched dogs galumphing for balls or waiting at the shore for their owners to return from a swim.

As Rebecca Giggs writes in her essay on Covid-19, plagues 'derange the senses in a symptomology that gallops ahead of the infection'.[1] She refers to the bird-faced masks worn during the Great Plague of London, the last major epidemic of bubonic plague, which originated in the Black Death of 1346 to 1353 and decimated Europe. Giggs describes them as 'PPE from a time before the word "virus" existed' as it was believed, erroneously, that the plague was 'transmitted by "miasma" – foul odours released by rotting organic matter and sewage'.[2] To protect themselves, doctors wore cones stuffed with herbs such as lavender and camphor and strapped them over their noses. They also wore a head wrapping beneath the mask and goggles to cover their eyes, forcing their attention to the olfactory. Meanwhile, those who were concerned about contracting an infection 'might also carry sponges soaked in vinegar to whiff, or place fragrant oranges pierced with cloves around the home'.[3] During that fourteenth-century plague, people mediated the world through smell.

*

Smell is one of the ways, in the absence of hearing, that I orient myself. When living with flatmates, I can't hear when they get up in the mornings, but I can smell their shampoo and the coffee on the stove.

On the farm, my smellscape was like light and dark. Sometimes the dogs would hit the jackpot and find a sheep carcass in a paddock.

'Dad!' I complained. 'The dogs have rolled in something dead!'

I could tell where the cat had been by his fur: under the shearing shed if he smelled of sheep shit, or warming himself on a flat rock if his fur carried the sweet smell of lichen.

The smell of wattle was a thick, fragrant reminder that the cold and grey of winter were on their way out. The Banksia rose, wrapped around the water tank stand, would soon froth with blossoms of pale lemon, their scent percolating through the verandah to my parents' bedroom, where I sat at the piano, practising scales. Then came the smell of storms. In dry periods, some plants exude an oil which is captured by clay-based soil and rocks. When rain falls, the soil opens, releasing the oils and another compound called geosmin, which together make the smell of petrichor.

Once I watched my grandmother, who spent most of her adult life on the farm and knew its seasons intimately, press her nose against the window gauze when rain began to fall after a dry spell. She was smiling.

*

Covid-19 strips some infected bodies of their sense of taste and smell. Anosmia, hyposmia, ageusia and hypogeusia – a complete loss of, or reduced sense of, smell or taste – are all symptoms of the virus. In a meta-analysis (the synthesis of data from a range of studies), 12.2 per cent of study participants experienced a complete loss of smell more than twelve weeks after infection.[4] Our limbic system – which regulates emotions such as fear and pleasure, and drives such as hunger and sex – evolved from the olfactory cortex, which means that well-being and smell are closely entwined.[5] Given these connections, researchers are now starting to investigate the impacts of Covid-19 on well-being.[6] Meanwhile, another meta-analysis indicates that 3 per cent of patients have reported experiencing hearing loss and 4.5 per cent have experienced tinnitus after a Covid-19 infection.[7]

As of 13 April 2024, when it stopped tracking due to a lack of reported data, the Worldometer, an online site of world statistics run by a team of developers, researchers and volunteers, reported almost 705 million cases of Covid-19. Although a large number would not have been reported, due to asymptomatic cases, some 21 million people would likely have experienced hearing loss. Imagine all of Australia, minus the city of Sydney, having trouble with hearing. It's enough to make, in poet Ilya Kaminsky's words, a 'Deaf Republic'.[8]

Those who contract Covid-19 often find themselves facing a tailwind of fatigue. Even three months or more after diagnosis, approximately one third of people contended with persistent fatigue and more than one fifth demonstrated cognitive impairments.[9] This suggests that millions would have experienced the heavy fog of fatigue that can come with deafness.

As someone who is not fluent in Auslan, communicating is exhausting. I watch people's lips and eyes to read what they are saying, and I match what I think they are saying with their intonation and body language. To a nondisabled person the process seems effortless, and most people forget I am deaf within two minutes of my telling them. Mostly, I can't be bothered with reminding them because it consumes more energy. Added to this is the chronic anxiety of never knowing if I will be able to hear someone, of not realising a person is speaking to me, or of having to ask people to speak clearly and getting an adverse response. I am always pushing myself into the world of the hearing, and always accommodating, because assertion takes effort too. The combination of intense concentration, anxiety and effort means that my mind is often woolly.

*

In the silence of Covid-19, my body loosened. I didn't have to be alert to people walking up behind me or speaking to me. Usually, I don't feel this sense of comfort until I get home from work, worn out from a day of tensing my body in anticipation of receiving and decoding sound. I can take out my hearing aid, pour myself a gin and tonic, eat some crackers and sit down with a novel.

When getting to know Deaf writer Fiona Murphy as she wrote *The Shape of Sound*, I realised that she also experiences this lurch between tension and release. She writes, 'Mornings feel fresh with potential. My mind feels vigorous and wanders, unrushed and unencumbered. It is in these moments that I feel like I can *think*, rather than react or recoil.'[10]

Once while talking to Fiona over Zoom, I proposed that what we might be feeling is 'Deaf Time', when we can simply be deaf, and be ourselves.

*

Before I left for Munich, I saw a chronic fatigue specialist to try to work out what was wrong with my body, because I was constantly tired and ill with bouts of flu. The specialist couldn't find the usual markers of chronic fatigue, though she acknowledged that I was clearly exhausted. In the months following my move to the holiday house on the coast when I returned from Munich, I worked through my fellowships remotely and wrote essays and conference papers. Although I was still typing up my corrections before the television in the evenings, I didn't have to contend with the strain of teaching as well. I was in Deaf Time, and my body began to heal.

Deaf Time could be considered a variant of Crip Time which, unlike linear time, as denoted by the ticking of a clock, moves beyond traditional indications of success such as career, marriage and children. It can mean slowness – for example, in terms of taking longer to do activities – or quickness, in terms of the swift thought processes that many disabled people use when problem-solving. In short, 'crip time is about flexible time'.[11]

Deaf Time, more specifically, means pausing and allowing meaning to unfurl. Once, in Melbourne, I stepped out in a long green-and-pink dress, and passed several people as I headed for the pedestrian crossing. Waiting for the lights to change to green, a series of words coalesced in my head, and I registered that someone had spoken to me.

'That's a nice dress,' they said.

I turned to a man nearby who, I saw now, was looking at me, eyebrows raised with expectation.

'Thank you! Nearly everyone is wearing black, so I thought I'd put on something bright.' I smiled at him and crossed the road.

Another time, a fellow deaf colleague, presenting at a symposium, stumbled over his words. He apologised afterwards, explaining, 'You might have noticed I had a real deaf moment. The subtitles covered the words on my screen, so I couldn't follow what I was reading. Luckily I had my hard copy.'

I laughed and assured him it wasn't a problem. I recalled him pausing, and I liked that he had called it a 'deaf moment' – a space to work out where and when he was.

*

In March 2024, four years after the terrible journey home from Munich, I sat at a desk in a modest suburban house at 32 Albert Street, Cabramatta. The window before the deck looked out to a quiet road, where a few cars passed by. The house had belonged to Gough Whitlam, prime minister from 1972 to 1975. I was hosted by Varuna, the Writers' House, and the Whitlam Institute at the University of Western Sydney.

One morning my fellow resident Kath and I walked to the Holiday Inn, formerly the Cabramatta Sunnybrook Motel. Kath approached the front desk and asked if they knew anything of the hotel's history. 'Gough Whitlam found out he won the election here.' The young woman behind the desk looked nonplussed.

Whitlam's biographer Jenny Hocking recounts how he and his supporters were crammed into Room 7 of the hotel, watching the television. At 10.30pm, he emerged from the room with his wife Margaret, 'greeted the press throng outside, poured the (Australian) champagne and joined them'.[12] When Billy McMahon conceded defeat, Whitlam, his office staff, campaigners and Margaret walked back up the hill to Albert Street, passing hundreds of supporters lining the street and shouting his name.

The house was 'surging with people streaming in to celebrate, to watch the tally on the television sets scattered around the garden, to see Gough Whitlam. Hundreds of chanting, cheering party-goers rushed towards him.'[13] After twenty-three years of Liberal-Country Party rule, it was time for a change.

At the residency, in the late afternoon, I hung up one of my hand-washed frocks on Margaret's Hills hoist. I found it hard to imagine this small, quiet backyard – with a pink dusk softening the suburban skyline beyond – crammed with boisterous supporters, laughing, swilling beer and watching the telly on the lawn.

*

I found a walking route along Cabramatta Creek that led to the Georges River. To reach it, I dashed through a gap in the busy Hume Highway traffic, then walked the perimeter of an oval. Along the creek, and then the river, I passed people walking, playing soccer, fishing, and powering toy boats with remote controls. Further out, on the water, were real-life yachts.

It was three months since my mother had died and I was still exhausted, so I was glad for the chance to wander, as I had as a child on the farm. I would drag a stick behind me as I walked to my grandmother's, feeling the vibrations of it rattling on the gravel road. My brother cycled on his BMX bike along the paddocks' levee banks, singing and whistling. My sister, walking back from the piggery when she was five or six, was so intensely involved in her thoughts that she didn't notice the snake warming itself on the ground until she stood on it. When she reached the house and told our parents, they were surprised she was still alive. They peered at the puncture marks in her jeans and figured it was either a dry bite, or that the denim had stopped the fangs from piercing her skin.

These days everyone is watching their screens. Sometimes, on the bus, I force myself to stop playing Words with Friends or laughing at dog videos on Instagram, so that I look out the window and allow myself to become bored.

*

During the pandemic our world quietened, folding in on itself. Planes stopped flying overhead, penguins waddled down empty pavements, sediment in rivers settled without the disturbance of boats, showing us what happens when we stop rushing. We lost much: loved ones, the ease of travel, secure jobs and futures. But we also gained something that couldn't be grasped in the frenzy of pre-pandemic consumption: a condition of stillness and watchfulness.

Would a return to Deaf Time, to deaf moments, to the time of Covid-19 and the time of childhood, help with slowing down? Would resting, rather than extracting, encourage us to lead sustainable lives? Would working out where and when we are in time enable us to take stock and do something about the climate crisis?

Yes, I think, it would. It's deaf-initely time.

Hostile Architecture

The spikes on London's window ledges, used to keep pigeons away, are 'hostile architecture'. The term applies to humans as well. In 2014, an image posted to Twitter went viral. It showed a small cement alcove in a high-end, brick apartment block in South London. Small silver cones studded the alcove, making it impossible for a homeless person to sleep there comfortably.

The public outcry was so strong that within a week the building's management had removed the studs, even though placing them in the alcove had not broken any laws because it was private property.[1] As scholars have commented, this kind of 'defensive' or 'disciplinary' architecture is designed to make itself unusable. It is also designed to exclude particular people, such as those without homes, from public places.[2] Other examples of hostile architecture include the Camden bench, installed by Camden's local council in London in 2012. Deaf writer and science communicator Frank Swain describes it as a 'pale, amorphous lump of concrete [that] is designed to resist almost everything in a city that it might come into contact with'.[3] It is coated with a substance that repels graffiti, is too uncomfortable for people to sleep on, and its tilting sides repulse skateboarders. It is, Swain observes, intended to be used as anything except a bench, which makes it a 'strange artifact, defined far more by what it *is not* than what it *is*. The Camden Bench is a concerted effort to create a non-object'.[4]

*

Early in my academic career, I was concerned about making myself employable. My contract was not permanent and jobs in academia, particularly in the humanities, were scarce. I took on some teaching for experience, even though I knew it would be difficult.

When I was a student, I used an FM system to hear in class. A teacher wore a transmitter, a small box with a microphone attached to it. I wore the receiver, which was another box attached to a loop around my neck. It captured the sound of the teacher's voice and carried it to my hearing aid. After fifteen years of service the wiring wore out, and I patched it up with sticky tape. I was still using this system when I became an academic, and the wires crackled as they transmitted sound.

It was much harder for me to function as an academic than as a student, because instead of listening to one person (a teacher), I had to focus on a plethora of voices. I asked the students to raise their hands when they wanted to speak, because I couldn't locate where their voices were coming from. I could only hear one voice at a time, which meant that we rarely held fast-paced discussions. Although the conversation was slower and the students, waiting for the microphone, had time to think before they spoke, I still needed to be quick on my feet. I would ask a question, locate a hand, move towards the student and stand near them with the microphone, listen to their answer, think of a response and ask another question, all the while doing the usual cognitive processing of lip-reading, matching the sound to words, checking the context to ensure I'd heard the right words, and piecing sentences together. By the time I reached home, I was white with fatigue.

When I was new to this process, my body became run-down from the strain and anxiety of hearing. I was constantly beset by colds and flu. My coughing kept Bruce awake at night and I spent most weekends in bed, recovering. Eventually, one of my colds resulted in an ear infection.

'It hurts!' I wailed to Bruce, crouching over and leaning my forehead on the carpet. He suggested something to do with a bowl and steam, but I couldn't concentrate on what he was saying. The pain suddenly subsided and fluid trickled down my earlobe. I realised my eardrum had ruptured.

'Do you think it will get infected over night?' I asked.

'Probably not.'

The next morning, I went to the doctor for antibiotics.

For a month I was completely deaf. I realised it wasn't worth losing my remaining hearing over my job. By law, employers are required to make reasonable adjustments that accommodate their disabled employees, but as Fiona Murphy has written in her *Overland* essay 'Reasonable Adjustments', this is by no means a given:

> After dedicating years of scholarship to workplace accessibility, in 2015 David Baldridge from the College of Business at Oregon State University summed up all the available research: 'Simply put, people with disabilities appear to face a straightforward yet troubling question, "if I ask for a needed accommodation, will I be better or worse

off?"' This question, I realise, has become so innate, so reflexive, that I can't even imagine what it would be like to not have to calculate risk. My fear feels corporeal, so full of consequence.[5]

As an academic early in their career, I too was frightened of asking for accommodation. I wanted to reduce my teaching hours to alleviate the strain on my body, but I didn't know if this was possible. After I made some enquiries, the university allowed me to reduce my hours to give my body more time to heal, but this meant taking a pay cut. Eventually, I left that job in search of more humane employment conditions.

*

In *The Shape of Sound*, Fiona Murphy meditates on Winston Churchill's comment, 'We shape our buildings and afterwards our buildings shape us,' uttered in 1943 as he surveyed the wreck and subsequent repair of the House of Commons after it was bombed in the Blitz. Others suggested that the new chamber be built in a horseshoe, or circular arrangement, as Australia's parliament is laid out. However, Churchill maintained that the original pattern of the parliament – what he referred to as an 'adversarial rectangular pattern' – should be upheld. Murphy notes that at the time Churchill made his comments on the parliamentary chamber, his hearing loss was starting to have an impact on his life. Her observation is a stroke of insight, like light pouring through clouds. She comments, 'Perhaps Churchill's arguments for retaining a "confrontational design" were motivated by wanting to retain the historical ties to British democracy, but it seems no mere coincidence that his recommendations benefitted someone who was hard of hearing.'[6] She observes that the Commons Chamber is narrow enough to read lips. Churchill's hearing loss might have had some bearing on British democracy.

If our buildings shape us, what kind of students, and what kind of academics, are our institutions creating? In the whole time that I have been an undergraduate, a postgraduate and an academic, I have seen no more than a few students in wheelchairs, two other deaf students and two blind academics. There would have been many more, as most impairments are invisible, but I cannot help but ask: where are all the disabled people in our universities?

While research is emerging on the experiences of disabled academics in the United Kingdom and United States, evidence of their experiences in the Australian academy is 'sparse and opaque'.[7] A pilot project surveying disabled academics in Australia, which included interviews with eight participants, revealed three key themes: the expectation of the 'ideal worker', which is impossible for disabled people to achieve except at a huge physical and mental cost; expectations of work performance and output that have intensified in the neoliberal university, which is challenging for disabled academics; and a disjunct between the policy and the practice of inclusion.[8] Just as I worked until I ruptured my eardrum, so too did some of the participants in this study drive themselves to 'achieve the norm of the ideal worker'. They did this by 'pushing themselves, often beyond capacity'.[9]

The universities I have inhabited were built largely for privileged, white, able bodies. A friend, reading a piece I had written about the beautiful, creamy sandstone blocks of a wealthy, established university, pointed out that they were also built on the extraction from Country. Australia's first universities were, after all, created for the children of wealthy immigrants. These days, they run on free labour, with academics often working unpaid hours to maintain their research. Disabled academics, in particular, extend their hours of work, and work more intensely in their standard hours, to achieve the same as their nondisabled counterparts.[10]

*

Gallaudet University is one of two universities for deaf people in the United States (the other is the National Technical Institute for the Deaf in Rochester). It utilises the concept of DeafSpace, which uses space, acoustics and colour in ways that benefit deaf people. DeafSpace was developed by architect Hansel Bauman, American Sign Language storyteller Ben Bahan, and Dr H-Dirksen Bauman, a Deaf Studies scholar at Gallaudet University.[11]

Hansel Bauman took notes on architectural conditions that enable deaf people to function well: conversation circles that allow clear sightlines so that everyone can see one another's lips and hands; diffused light sources that minimise contrast and backlighting (which make it difficult to lip-read); soft corners that allow deaf people to see who is coming, rather than banging into them because they can't hear an approach.

Bauman also drew on behaviour in deaf groups to demonstrate that a building can act as a third person – the third person who looks out for and cares for deaf students. If deaf people are having a conversation, someone will look out for traffic that they may not otherwise see because they are concentrating on people's faces and hands (and I have fallen in the gutter before, because I was lip-reading rather than watching where I was going). DeafSpace is, Bauman writes, 'empathy translated into built form'.[12]

*

A highlight of my time at primary school was the school fete, held over winter. I hovered near the vat of oil bubbling with doughnuts, the air heady with the scent of cinnamon. In the afternoon were the races. We stepped into hessian sacks and bounced forward over the grass, or placed an egg in our grandmothers' dessert spoons and dashed ahead, the egg wobbling. One or two dropped and smashed, egg yolk and albumen stretching across the grass. My brother, who was a good sprinter, often came out ahead, egg still intact.

For the three-legged race, I grabbed my brother, a cousin, or a schoolfriend. I slid my right foot, and they their left foot, into a thick band of black rubber. A teacher or parent stood near the starting line, and Mrs Woodley, my teacher, was next to them with a large white handkerchief held high above her head. When the pistol fired, she dropped her hand. I never had the heart to tell her that I could always hear the gun.

My brother and I were off, striding in time at first, then laughing as we veered out of sync. Beneath my laughter simmered a film of panic. I should have been able to move steadily, and was unnerved that the weight of another body, a leg stepping out of time with mine, meant I couldn't stay the course.

To win a three-legged race, one needs to sync with the person your leg is tied to. Running a three-legged race as a deaf writer in academia means that, to succeed, I need the support of colleagues and managers. In recent years this has been gifted to me, and I have thrived. When the person I am running with ignores me, or expects me to work like a nondisabled person, I stumble and fall.

*

What is my DeafSpace? I dream of small classes with captioning, rooms with good acoustics, and of having enough time and funding to become fluent in Auslan. Of time to think deeply, instead of churning out publications for points and promotion. These dreams, and the dreams of other disabled people, would benefit not just us. One of the tenets of Universal Design is that design for disabled people benefits everyone (for example, kerbs for wheelchairs also help people with prams, and soundfield systems make teachers' voices clear for all students in a classroom, not just those who are deaf or hard of hearing).

I dream, too, of a house full of light, with long, unbroken rooms so that I can always find Bruce. The floorboards are old trees underfoot, warm from the sun. Velvet couches for resting and reading. Mohair rugs and cashmere jumpers. A friend coming around for tea and biscuits. A dog who is soft to stroke, who alerts me when the friend is at the door. A place of sunlight and gentleness.

Intertwining

The light on Solway Firth in Cumbria was silver, slung low across the water. Although it was mid-morning, within a few hours the sun would slip beneath the horizon. My friends and I scrambled over rocks weathered by the wash of tides. I was wearing thermals, two jumpers, a red beanie and a coat, but the wind flew from the sea through my layers. My teeth clattered. We clambered around a corner, where we could just see Scotland on the other side of the firth. I wondered if Georgiana Kennedy ever stood where I was, before she became Georgiana Molloy and left England in 1829. Would she have smelled brine sweeping from the sea, her gaze drifting east over the salt marshes green with flat sedge, channels of water running between them? If she had lifted her eyes, would she have seen a flock of starlings spiralling?

*

In the Doe Library at the University of California, Berkeley, I knelt on the carpet, peering at the book spines on the bottom of the stack. It was the Australian literature section, and I was looking for something to connect me to home during my year on exchange. My family was 12,000 kilometres away, and I was beginning to understand what it may have been like for my mother, who migrated from New Zealand to rural New South Wales to be with my father in the 1970s.

I pulled out a book patterned with dark red leaves, titled *An All Consuming Passion*, and read the blurb on the back. It was a biography of Georgiana Molloy.[1] Molloy and her husband were among the first wadjelas (white people) to encroach on Wadandi Noongar boodja in 1830. Following her son's death in 1837, she began collecting seeds and specimens for an English horticultural connoisseur, Captain James Mangles. Intrigued, and with my feet fizzing from pins and needles, I checked out the book.

It transpired that Mangles and the Kennedy and Molloy families had kept many of Georgiana's letters. I was drawn to her descriptions of plants in her letters to Mangles. 'I beheld a Tree of great beauty,' she wrote, 'the flowers are of the finest white, and fall in long tresses from the stem, some of its pendulous blossoms, are from three, to five, fingers in length, and these wave in the breeze like Snow wreaths.'[2] Later, I became entranced by the courage of a woman who left family and friends to travel 15,000 kilometres to the other side of the world. Despite immense heartbreak and hardship, she taught herself to identify and collect tiny seeds and specimens of south-west Western Australian flora, such as the starry white clematis, the red drops of kennedia, and the drosera, dappled with mucilage that looks like dew.

*

At Solway Firth, my friends and I climbed back into the car and drove along a narrow lane hemmed by dry-stone walls. I had made these friends when I lived in London while doing my PhD; they were part of a book club which we named the Book Rangers. They were now living in Newcastle, and when I mentioned my research to them, they offered to show me around the area in which Georgiana grew up.

We circled the nearby city of Carlisle, where Georgiana was born in 1805. Her father, an ambitious Scotsman named David Kennedy, had married Elizabeth Dalton, daughter of the Mayor of Carlisle. Keen to establish himself, Kennedy built a house on his wife's land (which was now his) at Crosby-on-Eden, a few kilometres east of Carlisle. Georgiana, as a girl training to become a lady of leisure, learned her first lessons about plants in its gardens. Like other decorative arts such as writing, painting and flower arranging, botany was perceived to be a worthwhile pursuit for women. As Ann Shteir writes in *Cultivating Women, Cultivating Science*, the study of botany encouraged women to go outdoors, learn botanical Latin and read handbooks about Linnaean systematics.[3]

Georgiana's father fell from his horse and died in 1819, leaving behind debts, five children and a widow with no means of supporting them. Georgiana was fourteen. As she grew older, her family situation became even more unstable. She clashed with her mother and sister, an alcoholic. In 1829, Georgiana married Captain John Molloy, who had fought in the Napoleonic Wars but found it difficult to establish himself afterwards, and determined to move to Australia. Although Georgiana was not certain about John or the prospect of leaving her friends and country, her career options – for marriage was a job and a means of accessing an income – were narrowing.

My friends and I drove past the River Eden, which flowed out to the firth. It had broken its banks with heavy rain; water shone on the saturated fields, reflecting bare alder trees. The next day would be my thirty-seventh birthday.

'Do you know,' I told my friends, 'tomorrow I'll be the same age as Georgiana when she died. She had seven kids and a miscarriage and I'm still trying to decide whether to have a baby.'

I thought about Georgiana's body, how she grew each child in her womb from a seed-like embryo and how, for all of the time she was in Australia, she was either pregnant or nursing. Her children absorbed her nutrients, her breast milk, her intellectual and emotional energy, and her time. She would have known how each of her children smelled, the pitch of their voices, and the feel of their delicate skin beneath her work-roughened hands.

It slapped me like a wave, this craving to hold a child in my arms. I steadied myself, waiting for it to roll by.

*

The Molloys' voyage to Australia was marked by death. A child of a fellow passenger died four days after his birth, his 'interior organs not being perfect from exhaustion', Georgiana wrote to her friend Frances Birkett in 1831.[4] One of John Molloy's horses aborted her foal; he lost all his pigs between England and the Cape; shearing sheep and lambs on board 'died daily'; Georgiana's raspberry, gooseberry and currant slips at first flowered in the heat, then died from it. She watched a hive of bees in a box she bought at Gosport, until they all died.[5]

On the ship, amidst the sweep and lull of waves and the dying bees, Georgiana read poetry by Robbie Burns and books about botany. She was ill from morning sickness and poor food, and struggled with the heat as they approached the tropics. When her headaches grew worse,

John cut her light-coloured hair, then carefully drew his razor from the nape of her neck up to the curve of her skull. She shivered from his touch and the fresh air on her neck and scalp.

A baby is a seed that takes nine months to germinate. It, too, needs sunlight, water and nourishment. On the ship, 'the poor animals had scarcely enough to live on' and Georgiana 'really was nearly starved and every day from the Cape to Swan River, had only Salt Pork and Rice, the mutton was diseased that Mr Semphill the Charterer bought at Cape Town'. Georgiana was 'weak with constant sickness' and needed support when she walked. She often fell, bruising herself.[6]

The Molloys arrived at Fremantle on 12 March 1830. Georgiana showed an immediate interest in her surroundings, examining the shrubs and trees, and finding them without flowers. After a boat trip with her husband up the Swan River to Perth, she described the country as 'beautifully wooded to the water's edge with both copse wood and magnificent old trees, large firs and bushes about six or eight feet high'.[7] The Molloys intended to settle around the Swan River but found there was no land left for taking. They sailed south to what the governor, James Stirling, named Augusta for Prince Augustus Frederick, the sixth son of George the Third, who had died ten years before after being worn down by blindness, deafness and mental illness.

Georgiana was by this stage heavily pregnant. On 24 May 1830, the day after her twenty-fifth birthday, she 'was confined when thinking nothing of the kind'. She wrote to Frances, 'I suffered 12 hours and had no medical man near me there being none within some hundred miles, when at a loss what to tell my female servant I referred to the Encyclopedia.' The baby who arrived was tall and delicate with 'beautiful fingers & nails'.[8]

The day after the birth, Georgiana found her daughter's dress soaked in blood because the umbilical cord hadn't been properly tied. A few days later, the baby had convulsions and her feet were icy. Tiny white spots like blisters dotted her tongue, her temperature veered between hot and cold, and she screamed relentlessly. Georgiana lay on a sofa, the only furniture they had, but would not let her daughter from her arms because she was concerned the baby would become chilled. In an undated and unaddressed account that lies in her archives, Georgiana chronicled that her baby was 'carried off by violent convulsions on the twelfth day. I sat up with her from two that morning until all was over.'[9] Outside the tent, it rained and thundered and, Georgiana wrote to her mother, she had to hold her 'dead infant's limbs to keep them straight'.[10]

Later, she wrote to Frances, 'I thought my brain was going, in a desolate land.'[11] To her mother, she was more explicit: 'I felt inclined to rush out into the open air and charge the winds with what weighed so heavy at my bursting head.'[12] Georgiana's response was elemental, a fierce engagement with the natural world prompted by the most unbearable of circumstances.

Georgiana placed her daughter in a coffin at the foot of the sofa, there being no other place for the baby to rest. Then, to 'dispel the sad blank her death occasioned', she went out and planted bulbs.[13]

Sometime after her daughter's burial, Georgiana wrote in her undated account, 'Dear Molloy went unknown to me and sowed Rye Grass and Clover over [the grave] and has recently put some twigs across it to form a sort of trellice work with the surrounding creepers which in this country are very numerous.' Later, Georgiana planted clover, mignonette and pumpkins, which would 'rapidly creep on the twigs over it & form a sort of Dome'.[14] Her touching rendition of the Australian creepers mingling with English plants – and being given support to do so – suggests that Georgiana had tentatively embraced her environment.

When her daughter was buried in the Australian soil, Georgiana also buried a part of her body she had nurtured for nine months. As Barry Commoner, one of the founders of the modern environmental movement, explains in *The Closing Circle: Nature, Man and Technology*, 'everything must go somewhere'. This was the first of his four rules regarding ecology. He maintained there is no 'waste' in nature and there is no 'away' to which things can be thrown.[15] Perhaps because her child had been absorbed by the soil, and that soil sprouted delicate, long-limbed spider orchids and blushing outbreaks of pink everlastings, Georgiana could not help but love it.

*

In my early twenties, my body set up a persistent clamour for the feel of a soft head of hair beneath my chin, and a sticky finger circling my forefinger, but my chances of meeting someone to conceive with were slim. Although I could interact relatively well with one person at a time, I was awkward in company, fearing to speak in case I misheard or spoke out of turn and embarrassed myself.

I found it more rewarding to pursue writing and ideas than people who made me feel uncomfortable. Those ideas took me to London in my late twenties where, absorbed by my research and writing, I ignored my longing for a child. When I returned to Australia, I was tired of being on my own and, gritting my teeth against my discomfort, I pulled out all the stops to find a partner. When I met a dark-haired, brown-eyed former ecologist studying for a degree in philosophy, I was four years shy of forty.

The start of a relationship is like building an ecosystem, setting up a symbiosis of bacteria, conversations, oxytocin after sex. After a few months with this man, whose pale skin was dotted with moles and who shared my love of science, philosophy and writing, I was enmeshed, reliant on another organism.

Sitting on the couch one evening, drinking red wine, I asked, 'Do you want to have kids?'

His answer was emphatic. 'No.'

I held myself still, trying not to react. 'Why?'

'It's selfish.'

'What? Parents love their children. They're endlessly generous. How can that be selfish?'

'The child doesn't get to have a say in being born.'

I blinked. This had never occurred to me. I chewed on the thought, then tried again. 'So you don't want to have them?'

'No.'

My tears came in a hot, unexpected rush.

*

As the colony at Augusta established itself, Georgiana bore another two daughters, Sabina and Mary, and a son, John. In 1836, she received a letter from Captain James Mangles, a London horticulturalist whose cousin, Ellen Stirling, was the wife of the then-governor of Perth. A box of English seeds accompanied the letter. Mangles, caught up in the craze for exotic – at least to British eyes – Australian flora, wrote to request the exchange of English seeds for 'the Native Seeds of Augusta'.[16] Georgiana had expected to be able to collect specimens for herself, as in a letter to Mangles she referred to a *hortus siccus*, a book into which dried specimens were fastened, which she had brought with her to her new home 'imagining [she] should have a superfluity of time to use it'.[17] However, her superfluity was taken up by what she described to him as 'domestic drudgery' and she largely put off the collecting.[18]

Towards the end of that year her son, nineteen months old, wandered off after breakfast, fell into a well and drowned. Overwhelmed with grief once more, Georgiana wrote an impassioned letter about the child's death to Mangles, a man she had never met. She described how 'that lovely healthy child who had never known pain or sickness and who had been all mirth and joyousness five previous hours the last time we beheld him together was now a stiff corpse, but beautiful and lovely, even in death'.[19] As with her first child's death, when she placed blue flowers on her child's grave, Georgiana distracted herself by turning to the natural world. She embraced Mangles' request to collect seeds, writing in the same letter, 'Since my dear Boy's death I have daily employed myself in your service.'[20]

Mangles, a member of the Royal Society and co-founder of the Royal Geographical Society, sent Georgiana's specimens to his contacts, which included the Loddiges nurserymen of Hackney; Joseph Paxton, gardener at Chatsworth and designer of the Crystal Palace for the

1851 Great Exhibition; and John Lindley, the first professor of botany at University College London. By distributing her seeds in this way, Mangles cemented his social and professional ties with these men. They classified and renamed the plants using the Linnaean system, grew them in their gardens and, once they had propagated, sold them to the public.

Georgiana could not name the plants she found, not officially, as it was almost impossible for women of the late eighteenth and early nineteenth centuries to participate in the institutions which formalised botanical science. With the exception of Margaret Cavendish in 1667,[21] they could not attend meetings of the Royal Society. Sensitive to her lack of authority, Georgiana wrote to Mangles on 8 July 1840, 'I send two flowers of the... I dare not say what, Dr Lindley must determine.'[22] John Lindley was the chair of botany at University College London from 1829 to 1860, and Mangles sent a number of Georgiana's seeds to him.

Undeterred by her lack of formal scientific knowledge, Georgiana developed her own system, whereby she gave each flower and its seed a number. She asked Mangles to 'oblige me by sending me the names of the different flowers according to their numbers; I have kept the numbers of each, and the duplicates of most of the Specimens that I might have the satisfaction of hearing some name attached to them'.[23] Although she might not have been aware of it, Georgiana was practising science: she created and organised her knowledge of the plants, then tested her knowledge against that of other scientists. As she worked, she developed a sense of purpose and vocation, and in 1840 she wrote to Mangles, 'when I sally forth either on foot or Horseback, I feel quite elastic in mind and Step; I feel I am quite at my own work, the real cause that enticed me out to Swan River'.[24]

*

Although infant mortality was common well into the twentieth century, the death of Georgiana's children would never leave her. I knew this, and felt for her deeply as she sat in that tent, holding her dead daughter while a storm bashed through the karri trees beyond, because my parents lost their first son when he was eight months old. Although they came to grips with their grief and moved on with their lives I, a sensitive child who was alert to all that was unspoken, sensed the lacuna he left in our family. Despite this, I still wanted to have children.

Twice more, when I'd had too much red wine with Bruce, I brought up the subject. Each time, the answer was no. Each time I burst into tears, surprised by their velocity.

I began to weigh things up. I was thirty-eight. I had enough time to leave and find someone else before I became infertile, but it had taken five years of terrible dates to connect with someone who delighted me so much. Even if I left, there was no surety that I could conceive.

Besides, he had become part of my ecosystem, sustaining me with his knowledge and wit. In his presence I unfurled like petals stretching open to the sun. If I uprooted myself I'd wither, becoming desiccated.

*

The stands of karri rose so far above my head I could have been underwater. Among the tallest trees in the world, they are 50 to 60 metres in height. I stood at the base of a fine, straight trunk in the Boranup forest. Most of this forest was logged in the late nineteenth century, but the trees had grown again. The light falling through the canopy was speckled, the way it is when you swim in the sea and look up, watching it fall like flecks of gold. The karri trees are native to this wet corner of the south-west, and they tower over a thick, bright-green understorey of ferns and tassel flowers. The air was cool on my bare arms.

Arriving in Fremantle in 1830, Georgiana found 'the Country itself an unlimited extent of dark green wood'.[25] Like many others, she assumed that soil with plenty of trees meant it was fertile for English crops. She wrote, 'on the coast as usual there is much sand, but here it is fruitful and you can see the immense timber growing from it'.[26] Georgiana's words indicate how poorly the Europeans understood their new environment, for the landscapes in Western Australia are among the oldest and most weathered in the world and the soil is light on nutrients.

Despite this, colonisation crept across the south-west like a parasitic vine, drawing upon the labour of Wadandi Noongars and their country. Wadandi Noongars took livestock not only as rent payments for the illegal occupation of their land but also as food sources. Hostility between Wadandi Noongars and colonists began to increase. In 1841 Gaywal, whose home was at Wonnerup, speared colonist George Layman in an argument over damper and, more generally, his occupation of Gaywal's country. John Molloy, then the resident magistrate, and his neighbours the Bussells, led a punitive party and massacred Wadandi people.

Georgiana was implicated in the process of colonisation by sending plants to Mangles. The plants, renamed by John Lindley, were part of a linguistic displacement that echoed the violent dispossession of Wadandi Noongars.[27]

Wadandi and Bibbulmun Noongars have been part of the south-west's ecosystem for at least 40,000 years, developing an intimate and intricate knowledge of the area's weather, soil, water, vegetation, and breeding and blossoming times, in addition to practising sophisticated mosaic-burning regimes that created grasslands to attract game for hunting. As Bruce Pascoe demonstrates in *Dark Emu*, First Nations peoples across Australia also practised animal husbandry, food storage and harvesting.[28] Theirs is a deep and abiding relationship that recognises responsibility for the ecosystems that ensure human and nonhuman survival.

When colonisers put an end to mosaic burning in the south-west, the vegetation thickened, smothering ground-layer plants which had relied upon light and air to flourish. Tree clearing also created islands of habitat that lost their connectivity to that ecosystem, diminishing the diversity of plant and animal life in the islands. Andy Chapman, a zoologist who carried out fieldwork in the 1970s, found that clearing affected small perching birds. They didn't have enough energy to fly long distances and were accustomed to existing within very specific but connected areas. As Bill Bunbury writes in *Invisible Country*, his compilation of stories and oral histories about the changes in the environment in the south-west, a country broken up by clearing makes it challenging for these birds to grow their populations.[29]

Another of Commoner's rules is 'Nature knows best'. Humans, Commoner argues, have fashioned technology in the belief that it will improve upon nature. He rejects this, maintaining that major human-made change in a natural system is likely to be detrimental to it. This is evident from the large-scale tree clearing in the south-west, which means less transpiration – where plants or leaves give off water vapour – which in turn results in a drier atmosphere. Changes wrought by technology and colonisation are manifesting in the climate. Tony

Birch writes in *Unstable Relations*, 'Any discussion and analysis of climate change today must include an investigation of colonial history and its devastating impact on Indigenous nations.'[30]

Standing beneath the luminous stands of karri trees, I felt the hairs on my forearms bristle.

*

Georgiana laboured through seven pregnancies and a miscarriage, her body becoming weaker after each birth. She died at thirty-seven from puerperal fever after the arrival of her seventh child. The biological and cultural compulsion to breed killed her. It may well be a metaphor for how we are destroying ourselves.

The weathered soils of Australia, the driest inhabited continent on earth, were never meant to sustain large numbers of humans. If our population continues to grow without curbing its current rates of resource consumption, it will place increasing strain upon ecosystems. As Richard Monastersky writes in *Nature*, predictive models based on the current rate of extinction show that a mass extinction, defined as the loss of three quarters of all species, could occur over the next few centuries.[31] With extinction comes the loss of the natural support systems that keep us alive. Or, as Commoner puts it, there's no such thing as a free lunch.

*

When the third conversation about having a child ended in tears, I realised I had to either leave my relationship or change my thinking. I talked to friends as I worked out what to do.

'Having a baby is like throwing a bomb into your relationship,' said one.

'If your bloke doesn't support you, it will be bloody hard to write,' said another.

I watched my friends with their children. In the couples, which were predominantly heterosexual, women seemed to do the bulk of the child caring and had little time to themselves. As a writer, I knew this would drive me spare. While I understood that, unlike Georgiana, I lived in a culture that allowed me to make a choice about reproduction, I was still compromised by its inability to value the work of motherhood, or to let women reach their intellectual and artistic potential without enormous sacrifices.

I also realised, seeing how tired and stressed my female friends became as they changed into mothers, how much more stamina I would need to take care of a child, to listen out for them jamming a fork into the toaster. As a deaf woman, most of my energy is directed to trying to function in a hearing world. If a child was factored into that, there would be little left over for the man I loved. As he didn't want children, this was grossly unfair. I knew, too, that I'd never lose the fear of our child dying. My sister, who has three children and all her hearing, rose frequently at night when they were small to check they still breathed in their sleep.

Then I read a 2017 study by Seth Wynes and Kimberly Nicholas in *Environmental Research Letters*, which concludes that bringing another human into the world is one of the most destructive things a person can do to the environment.[32] The authors calculate that an American family choosing to have one fewer child would provide the same level of emissions reductions as 684 teenagers adopting comprehensive recycling for the rest of their lives. Meanwhile, the United Nations projects that 66 per cent of the world's population will live in cities by 2050, raising urgent questions about how these people are to be fed and clothed while pollinators such as bees are dying in massive numbers. If I had a child, they would be thirty by the time these issues erupted in earnest, while also contending with plastics travelling into our food chain and increasingly extreme environmental events such as droughts and rising seas. They're already happening for our neighbours in the Pacific.

I thought of the trees that promised such abundance for the Europeans in the south-west, how the soil in which they were rooted yielded so little once they were cut down. Survival in the twenty-first century lies, as First Nations peoples learned over tens of thousands of years, in careful attention to one's environment and what it can sustain.

The scales began to tilt.

*

The man I love stood on the rocks of Cape Freycinet, where the pale azure sky sloped into the sea. Before him, bolts of the ocean unfurled and slammed into the granite. Further back, where I was standing, a curve of boulders gathered the water to itself, soothing it into stillness. Here, the surface was aquamarine, so bright it was as though a consciousness glowed beneath.

This cape, some 40 kilometres north of where the Molloys lived, was named for French man Louis de Freycinet, commander of the *Casuarina* on explorer Nicolas Baudin's 1801 expedition to map the coast of Australia. The English, jealous of the French interest, stuck a flag in the sand at Albany and claimed Western Australia for their own, setting in train a spate of destruction.

Waves thrashed against the rocks, curling into foam. My dark-haired man turned away from the water and headed towards me, his sneakers gripping the gritty granite surface. Barry Commoner, once more: everything is connected to everything else. People overlook this, that their existence is predicated upon the dominance of an environment, upon nations that were enmeshed with their country in ecosystems that nourished them, and which nourish them still.

My longing for a baby will seep through my life, but if having a disability has taught me anything, it is that there are limits to my ability to support my art and a child, just as there are limits to the resources of our world. Although this saddens me, there are, undeniably, so many boons: time to write in rain-thickened air; golden light spilling across marri trees as the sun rises; the sharp smell of Christmas bugs burrowing in soil on December evenings; and this man walking towards me, sharply outlined against that vertiginous background of blue.

Swallows and Summers

Breda and I agreed to meet at the plastic tables beside the book tent in an interval at Adelaide Writers' Week. It's Breda's favourite writers' festival, and the seamless provision of Auslan interpreters makes it the most accessible. Since moving to Kaurna country for an academic job, I have tried to meet her at the festival every year.

After a session on book reviewing, I located my friend at a table. Breda is a historian and has been working on Deaf History Collections, an online collection of writing, images and artefacts created by deaf people.[1] It shows how deaf Australians have long congregated, established schools and used the written word to agitate for equality and justice. As academics, Breda and I have written work for each other's publications, and Breda launched my hybrid memoir *Hearing Maud* at Gleebooks in Sydney. At the table, we lip-read one another, I finger-spell and use some rough signs, and I can read some of Breda's signs, and together we hash out a conversation.

*

Virginia Woolf wrote in *A Room of One's Own* in 1929 that 'we think back through our mothers if we are women'.[2] In surveying her literary lineage, Woolf uncovers and draws attention to neglected female writers, arguing that literary precursors are necessary for women's capacity to write, and to sustain a writing career.

As I was raised oral deaf – that is, taught to speak and lip-read rather than sign – books were portals to other worlds. When I learned about deafness and the Deaf community, it was through reading.

I met Maud in the archive. She was born in 1874 in Queensland, and just before her parents were about to move the family to London, her mother found that Maud couldn't hear. In 1880, four years after they arrived in London, Rosa enrolled Maud in a school that forced her to lip-read and speak, often a more difficult mode of communicating than using sign language. However, it did mean that Maud became literate by learning to connect the words on people's lips with those on a page.

Writing then became another means for Maud to communicate with people. In the National Library of Australia in Canberra and in the John Oxley Library near Kurilpa, overlooking the Brisbane River, I followed Maud's careful cursive on delicate paper. She wrote letters to her grandfather Thomas Murray-Prior in Australia, her brother Humphrey in California, and to her mother when she was away travelling. In her late twenties, following the fragmentation of her family and her father's unexpected death, Maud had a breakdown. Her mother consigned her to an asylum in Surrey. Maud wrote a letter to her doctor asking to be released, which I found among her medical records in an archive in Woking. I realised that it was never posted. Indeed, Maud was never released from the asylum and outlived her entire family.

At the beginning of the records was an identification photograph. Maud looked tired, with shadows beneath her eyes. Her mouth was open, as if to speak.

*

Working in an archive, that place where manuscripts and other primary sources are kept, is a quiet business. Documents are held offsite in archival boxes that protect them from mice, ultraviolet light, mould and insects, which means that foot traffic, the rustle of turning pages, and conversations are minimal. I can hear if someone comes up behind me, so I don't need to be constantly alert. The floors are usually carpeted, which reduces reverberations. My intense focus on decoding words in cursive, or seeking a description of a plant or person, pushes away the constant churn in my brain.

It's how it used to be when I worked on my stamp collection as a girl. I sat, legs triangled, on the scratchy green carpet, sorting stamps according to size or year, then sliding them behind the strips of clear plastic in my album. Hunting for tiny dates to find the year they were printed, I could ignore the days at school when I sat alone, unable to start a conversation with anyone.

It's also easier for me to hear people in the archive. All I have to do is read their words, rather than focusing on lips or straining to hear sound.

*

In her memoir *Hysteria*, Katerina Bryant follows four women whose experiences of non-epileptic seizures have been similar or different to her own. She reaches back into time with the reasoning that, she writes, 'if I could find symptoms that matched my own, I would be able to find a cure. Instead I found ancestors – women throughout history whose strength and tenacity I am guided by.' Bryant wrote these words in an essay aligning *Hysteria* with *Hearing Maud*, in an approach that highlights the importance of connecting disabled women with their forebears in the archive. I did not realise it until I read Katerina's essay, but learning about Maud enabled me, to use Katerina's words, 'to see [my] own experiences of deafness within a history of disabled ancestors. For the disabled writer, it is worth noting that this encounter between subject and self is of higher stakes; our identities tie us together in understanding.'[3]

In Maud's writing to her family, I saw my own obsession with writing letters to find out about people's lives. When I was a girl, I wrote letters to my grandmother and great-aunt in New Zealand, my penpals in Singapore and my schoolfriends when they were on holidays. And as I learned about Maud's life, I learned more about how deafness had shaped my own life. Although we were born about a century apart and our lives went in radically different directions, many aspects were the same, such as our assimilation into the hearing world. I realised that the reverberations of the eugenics project of the nineteenth century continued into the late twentieth century. Maud had been taught to speak rather than sign because of the prevailing ideology that speech would lead to a hearing husband, and that their babies would be less likely to be deaf (even though the incidence of congenital deafness is very small). This emphasis on speech was still prevalent more than one hundred years later, and my parents, when I was diagnosed, lacked information on the importance of teaching sign language to deaf children. I also, in reading of Maud's closeness to her mother and her desperation to please those around her, saw myself, and felt less alone.

*

When I was fifteen, my father and his brothers – three strong farmers – wrestled the antique piano onto the back of the ute. They strapped it down with ropes and threw a table next to it. My mother loaded us into the car with suitcases and we moved from Gamilaroi country to Armidale, on Anaiwan country, following the ute as it trundled over gravel roads to Tamworth and the New England Highway. My father, who had painted watercolours since he was young, became an art teacher at the local boys' school. I became a day girl at the school where my sister and female cousins had boarded, but which had refused to take me because of my deafness. I learned that Judith Wright, one of Australia's most loved writers, had been a boarder at the school, finishing up in 1932. A number of her relatives were still there, with several Wrights on the roll.

Wright wasn't particularly happy at the school, which doesn't surprise me. My sister had been allowed home only twice a term. A bright and lively girl, she became unnaturally quiet as Sunday afternoon drew to a close. She sat in the beanbag in her uniform, silent, waiting for our father to take her to the bus.

I cannot recall at what point I discovered that Wright started becoming deaf in her mid-twenties from otosclerosis, a condition in which the three bones in the inner ear begin to harden, making it difficult for them to transmit sound. I started researching Wright's deafness seriously when I pitched an essay for Jessica Gildersleeve's *Routledge Companion to Australian Literature* in 2020. In my office, I consulted AustLit, the Australian literature database hosted by the University of Queensland. I searched for critiques about Wright's work and located only four sources that mentioned her deafness. Just one of these, by Susan Sheridan, contemplated Wright's deafness at length, in the context of her correspondence and friendship with blind artist Barbara Blackman. I sank back into my chair in disappointment. It seemed as if the whole of Australia's scholarly community had erased disability from its pages.

Although Wright never referred to her hearing loss in her poetry, she discussed it at length in an interview with Heather Rusden towards the end of her life, observing that deafness had 'reached into all the interstices of my life'.[4] Deafness clearly influenced her writing, underpinning one of her key themes – what scholar Kate Rigby refers to as 'negative poetics' – writing which sings the praises of the natural world, while at the same time acknowledging that there are limits to words' capacity to describe this world, or even to respond adequately to the way it summons us.[5] As a deaf person, Wright was aware of the limits of language. All it takes, in a conversation, is for someone to turn their head away so that one can no longer lip-read, and the conversation is over. For a deaf person who lip-reads, like Wright, language clearly has its limits, but Wright's critics have barely considered the impact of her impairment on her writing.

Wright was also a prolific correspondent because she found it hard to hear on the telephone, and three volumes of her letters have been published to date. Her deafness made her attentive to birds and animals, and her poems are rich with the colours and the flight trajectories of birds. The theme of *oikos* – the home, the habitat – often appears in her writing, and when Wright commented to Rusden that 'silence is my habitat', she was suggesting that deafness was a condition in which she felt at home.

However, when the interviewer commented that 'Deafness was a part of your life, yet you've chosen not to write about it', Wright replied, 'Oh, I wouldn't say it was a choice. I haven't felt it was an important part of my life in that way.'

Wright's claim that she never dwelled on deafness was not true. In 1967 she wrote a short book on Henry Lawson, published in Oxford University Press's 'Great Australians' series. When he was nine, Lawson became ill with earache and began to lose his hearing. In his autobiographical writings, which Wright had read, he describes the loss of his hearing as 'a thing which was to cloud my whole life, to drive me into myself, and to be, perhaps, in a great measure responsible for my writing'.[6]

In her book on Lawson, Wright observes:

> The deaf are forced into a kind of isolation, which often causes them to feel that the world is hostile or indifferent to them, and even to suspect that others are taking advantage of their misfortune to laugh at or criticise them in their own presence. They are cut off, too, from the ordinary occupations by the inability to share in conversations, and this drives them further into themselves. As Henry said, his deafness was probably a big factor in his writing; isolation spurs imagination.[7]

Unlike many other Australian literary critics writing on Lawson – Amanda Tink notes that only 10 of the 788 items on Lawson in AustLit acknowledge his impairment – Wright recognises Lawson's deafness and the impact it had on his writing.[8] She acknowledges that for a writer, deafness is not an impediment because of its intrinsic relationship with imagination and creativity. Silence can help writers to concentrate, after all. A fellow deaf author and academic, Scott, takes his cochlear off before he enters the space of thinking, reading and writing, and I always take out my hearing aid when I sit to write at my desk.

Wright's assertion that deafness wasn't something she chose to write about, while at the same time acknowledging that it reached into the crevices of her life, and had an impact on her creativity, is puzzling.

*

In 2010, at the University of Queensland, I sat at another plastic table, this time in the streaky shade of palms. It was warm, the humidity drawing sweat from my skin. Opposite me was Donna McDonald, a deaf woman writing her PhD on her own story of deafness.

I had moved to Brisbane the previous year after finishing my doctorate in London, and found a part-time job at Autism Queensland while writing my second novel. My boss knew Donna and mentioned that she was deaf. As always, I turned to words to find out more, reading Donna's essays on her website. I found much that resonated with me. In June 2010, I introduced myself to her in an email, writing, 'I found that I could identify with many of the things you wrote about in your essays – the sense of not really being in either the world of the hearing or of the deaf, your mother's love and hard work, and the isolation from other deaf people (I think I have only met about 2 or 3 other deaf people in my life).'

Born in the 1950s, Donna was first enrolled in a school that taught deaf children to speak. Afterwards, she attended a mainstream school where she excelled with lip-reading and hard work. Her determination led to achievements that proved her to be 'the deaf girl that had made good', as she wrote in her memoir.[9] Despite her focus on fitting into the hearing world, as she grew into adulthood, Donna realised that she missed her deaf schoolmates. She began to explore her and their deafness and how it shaped their lives. In reading her memoir,

I empathised with her experiences; for example, the panic that sets upon me in a blackout, when I can't see anything or lip-read anyone, and I lose my bearing in the world.

Donna is an artist as well as a writer, and the title of her memoir, *The Art of Being Deaf*, indicates that to live as a deaf or hard of hearing person in the world requires artfulness – that is, creativity and lateral thinking to respond to and solve problems.

Once we finished our coffees, Donna took me back to her office, where she gave me a print-out of her thesis draft, which included an analysis of representations of deafness in fiction. Many conversations later, she would ask me, 'Will you write about your deafness?'

I dismissed her suggestion. 'I don't think so. I know the subject matter so well that it doesn't challenge me.'

As I began to piece together *Hearing Maud*, however, I realised deafness was – as it had been for Wright – in all the gaps in my life. Although writing deaf characters was not interesting to me, the way it had led me to writing and influenced my craft was. Perhaps Wright, in her conversation with Rusden, was at the point that I had been in my conversation with Donna: unaware that we had been assimilated into the world of hearing people. Perhaps Wright had neither deaf friends nor deaf role models.

*

As I continued to write *Hearing Maud*, I realised that Australian disabled people needed a place to find their writing, just as Breda had created a space for deaf people to find their history. In 2018, while

I was on my postdoctoral fellowship, the AustLit database staff and I began to compile the Writing Disability in Australia dataset, with the aim of helping readers to find writing about specific impairments. Through this process, I was introduced to Patricia Carlon.

A writer of fourteen crime novels and several short stories, Carlon was profoundly deaf since age eleven, but her deafness did not become widely known until the end of her life. She communicated with her publishers via letters, refused interviews and did not disclose her impairment. As literary critic Susan Wyndham writes, the knowledge of Carlon's deafness 'came as a surprise to everyone else who knew "Miss Carlon", from her long-time London agent and her publishers in Melbourne and New York, to the woman who handled her money at the local bank every Friday'.[10]

Her nephew, a lawyer, observed that Carlon had 'a very small world'. As an adult, she lived in Bexley, a suburb not far from Botany Bay. She gardened, won local competitions with her cooking, and 'at one time was known as the cat lady of Bexley for all her feline companions'.[11]

Deaf playwright Sofya Gollan, when she was working with the Australian Theatre of the Deaf, wrote and acted in a play about Carlon, *The Cat Lady of Bexley* (2006). With a Deaf director, Caroline Conlon, Carlon's deafness was brought into the light.[12]

*

Although Carlon did not create deaf characters, her deafness shapes the plots and themes of her novels. In *The Whispering Wall* (1969) Sarah Oatland, a widow, has had a stroke. Completely immobilised, she can still see and hear but is unable to communicate. She listens to the doctor say to the nurse, 'Do you think she hears? She's laid out like a fish on a slab, with as much life to her, poor dear.'[13] Six weeks after Sarah's stroke, her mercenary niece Gwenyth announces that she is letting out parts of the house to tenants to raise money for Sarah's care. Four couples subsequently move in, including a mother with her daughter, Rose, and Mr and Mrs Phipps, a married couple who want to stay only a few months.

With her bed against the chimney wall, Sarah can hear voices travelling from the sitting room below. She learns, from arguments between Phipps and his wife, that they don't get along, and are only staying together because Phipps's inheritance depends on it. She also hears that Phipps intends to murder his father-in-law so that he can obtain this inheritance. Meanwhile, Rose, a clever and inquisitive girl, prompts Sarah to start communicating with her by blinking once for yes and twice for no. Sarah had previously tried to talk to Braggs, her nurse, like this, but she was slow because of her stroke and Braggs never waited for a blink.

The father-in-law visits and, through various communications, including blinking and using a Scrabble board, Sarah relays that she has overheard the Phipps's machinations. She realises that not only is the father-in-law's life in danger, but so is her own. Carlon deftly pulls all the characters and their relationships together, and at the crisis point Sarah, to save her life, is forced to call out.

As a deaf reader, I recognise a number of elements that were likely informed by Carlon's deafness. Although she could lip-read, she would also have been alert to alternative and inventive ways of carrying out conversations – as Sarah does through the Scrabble board. She would have been aware of the conditions she needed to communicate well, including the layout and architecture of rooms.

*

In *The Shape of Sound*, Fiona Murphy draws on the language of bodies – both human bodies and architectural bodies – to describe her experiences of deafness. She trained as a physiotherapist and, in learning the Latin and Greek terms for body parts, she found that the original words for body parts were also the names of everyday objects. Clavicle, for instance, comes from the classical Latin word *clavicula*, which means 'small key, bolt'. Once Fiona learned the origin of the words, she realised that 'the boundaries between our bodies and the world become permeable. Just as our bodies are named after commonplace items, our built world has taken on anatomical terms. A building can have good bones, there is the heart of a house, roads are the arteries of a city.'[14]

These observations on architecture and language stem not only from Fiona's training in physiotherapy, but also from her deafness. She can only hear well in certain spaces, as she writes: 'in these narrow spaces where walls meet, say in the corner booth of a café or backed up against the wall of a bar, that sound, at least for me, becomes articulate – the walls do the work of funnelling voices towards me, allowing speech to become distinct and clear. I am the space where I am: on the edges, cornered.'[15]

Fiona refers to something broader than architecture: the way her life had been corralled by the longstanding cultural denigration of disability, forcing her to hide her deafness, as Carlon did. Her sense of being cornered evokes Carlon's representation of Sarah trapped in her bed. The doctor and nurse, carrying out a conversation while oblivious to her presence, reminds me of the numerous times I have been unable to participate in group conversations, the many voices whirling above and beyond me.

In her memoir, Fiona also describes the weightiness of hiding her deafness. She writes, 'On the rare occasion when deafness or hearing loss was mentioned in school, I would seize up, as if holding my breath would somehow make me smaller and undetectable. With each passing school term, my fear of being found out intensified.'[16] Her fear manifested in her body, with 'sweat and spasms' whenever she imagined having to disclose her deafness.[17] Most days her body 'was visited by a quiet, tedious panic'.[18] Fiona's descriptions of secrecy, of passing and hiding, find a resonance in Carlon's novels. All fourteen novels are in the crime fiction genre, where there is always a secret that must be found out to resolve the crime.

When I hastened towards the end of *The Whispering Wall* and read how Sarah was forced to call out to save herself, I thought of the photo of Maud in the archives, her mouth open as if to speak. I thought of the deaf people who have written and signed, bringing their deafness into the open. For, as Fiona describes, the weight of a secret can make us ill.

Fiona's memoir, with its detailed attention to language, space and bodies, is at times a mirror for my own. Our lives have been distorted by the fatigue of passing as hearing; we were not born into Deaf communities but had to make our own way towards them; we both work relentlessly in our professions to develop some security in a world that is frequently hostile to deaf and disabled people. We use writing to speak about our experiences of deafness. Fiona is now a friend. In meeting her, I found my flock.

*

Donna writes about our encounter at the University of Queensland in *The Art of Being Deaf*, a book which was a beacon for Fiona and me. She reflects on our lack of deaf adult role models, largely because we were absorbed into hearing culture, and comments, 'I realise that one blue swallow does not make a summer.'[19] In other words, one connection between deaf writers does not make a tradition.

However, the swallows and summers are coming. McDonald's book, mine and Murphy's form a community of Deaf writers, one that connects with and reaches back to the words of Maud Praed, Judith Wright, Patricia Carlon, Sofya Gollan and Breda Carty. We seek our bodies in each other's words and find ourselves, reassuringly, reflected back. We are not outliers; we are part of a flock, and through writing we join those who have flown before us.

*

Adelaide Writers' Week is the only writers' festival at which I have been able to hear, in part because it is in a natural amphitheatre, shaded by trees. The festival also has loop systems, which help people with hearing aids to hear. The loop, or induction, system involves a string of wire set up around a particular area. A microphone picks up sound and transmits it to the wire. People with hearing aids can pick up the sound from the wire via a switch, known as a 'T-switch', on their hearing aid.

If the loop is working, the sound is gloriously clear, but to access it I need to sit in the area circled by the wire. In 2024, after a coffee with Breda, we found there were so many hearing people in the seats for deaf people that I had to ask the technical assistant if there was anywhere else I could sit.

'No, it's only that front section that has the loop wire around it. If you can't find a spot, I'll make an announcement and ask people to move.' He added, 'There are some very entitled people in Adelaide.'

I laughed and returned to Breda and her deaf friends at the front of the seating area, where they were sitting so they could see the Auslan interpreters. We managed to squeeze in because some of us – including Breda's husband, who is hard of hearing – sat on the ground. Together, we enjoyed Mary Beard's dry ripostes.

The Breath Goes Now

The blue gum had rooted itself in the black loamy soil hundreds of years before. Its thick girth was crusted with bark that sheltered ants and beetles. In summer it spread its long arms over the lawn, casting cool shade. In the evenings my brother, sister and I sprinted around its trunk in our thin cotton pyjamas, chasing the dogs. Occasionally we stabbed a bare foot on a twig and hopped, howling.

I grew up surrounded by chlorophyll. My mother inherited a green thumb from her father and spent weekends working with him in his garden in Christchurch. After finishing her Bachelor of Arts, majoring in History, at Canterbury University, she sailed across the ditch to Sydney with the intention of continuing around the world. However, she loved fashion, and her savings moved through her fingers like water as she pulled minidresses off the racks.

Eventually, she had to abandon her dreams of travelling and find a job. She worked at what is now the University of Technology Sydney, and not long after she met my father. Six months later, they married, my father wearing a navy Mr John by Merivale suit with an arrow in red stitching down the back. My father took my mother back to the family farm on Gamilaroi country in north-west New South Wales.

They moved into the worker's cottage next to the gum. Not long afterwards, they dug a hole at the base of the tree, placed a dead sheep in it for fertilisation, shovelled soil over the top and planted a pink jasmine seedling. Over the years, the vine grew vigorously, thickening and spreading over the tree's trunk.

As a child I lay awake at night, listening to the wind rush through the tree's leaves, breathing in the sweetness of the jasmine and eucalyptus carried through the open window.

*

A lung looks like an upside-down tree. When we breathe in air through our nose and mouth, it travels down our windpipe – the trunk of the tree – into the left or right bronchus. Smaller tubes, named bronchioles, branch off from each bronchus. At the end of the bronchioles are clusters of tiny sacs, known as alveoli, which are surrounded by blood vessels. When we inhale, oxygen passes through the paper-thin wall of the alveoli into the vessels and, when we exhale, carbon dioxide moves out.

Alveoli remind me of bunches of leaves, which work in a similar way: tiny holes in leaves, called stomata, draw in carbon dioxide and water. Using energy from the sun, they turn the carbon dioxide and water into glucose (a process known as photosynthesis), and the stomata release oxygen as a by-product.

*

When my mother was three, she was hospitalised with pneumonia. Penicillin was not yet widely available in Aotearoa, so she was treated with sulfa drugs and placed in an oxygen tent. It took her a long time to recover, and later the medical authorities found a tear in the tent. She went home to a house cloudy with cigarette smoke, with both parents smoking at least a pack a day. Her weak lungs meant she fell ill frequently throughout her childhood. My aunt told me that my mother coughed constantly as a teenager. My father relayed how, not long after he had met my mother, they sat on the headland at Bronte in Sydney. It was a mild evening, but my mother developed a chill, which turned into the flu.

Her cough became the backdrop of our lives, a watery gurgle that overtook her while she spread mulch on the vegetable beds or watched the news.

*

The blue gum sheltered possums, cockatoos, galahs, magpies and caterpillars. At its hollow base sat a pair of garden gnomes and, occasionally, my and my brother's Barbie dolls. My mother built garden beds of poppies and roses around it, as well as a rockery studded with succulents. Gardening may have been a way of orienting herself in rural Australia, a strange place after the ordered streets and gardens of suburban Christchurch.

When my brother, sister and I were small, our mother gardened so that we, forever in her orbit, would play outside. We washed soil from freshly tugged carrots under the tap next to the rainwater tank and picked strawberries before the day became too hot. In the orchard, while she bagged ripening nectarines to protect them from flying foxes, we were told to collect mulberries from the tree. We returned to the house with purple-stained mouths, our ice-cream containers only a quarter full of fruit.

On weekdays, our mother and father walked in the garden after breakfast with a cup of tea or instant coffee. They talked about the black spots on the rose bushes while the dogs lifted their legs against the fence posts, and we stuffed our schoolbags with lunchboxes and frozen water bottles. We raced out for a kiss goodbye and belted down the gravel road for the bus. Not long afterwards, my father drove out the gate in his ute or motorbike to work on the farm.

In the quietness of the day, my mother gardened, the possums slept, and bees hovered over the dark centres of the poppies.

*

My mother neared the end of her pregnancy with me during summer, when the heat stretched into the forties. Sweaty and heavy, she was fed up with waiting, so she went up to the piggery to help my father dig a trench, in the hope that her waters would break. Sure enough, as she wielded the pickaxe, they did.

Nearly four years after this event, I took ill with meningitis and lost my hearing.

As my father was busy farming, my mother drove me to appointments with the audiologist. On the three-hour round trip, she listened to the radio while I read books. The left side of my face developed more freckles than the right from the sun falling through the passenger-seat window. My mother, with her university major in history, also loved books, and on the car journeys we also talked about what I was reading.

These were the branches that held me firm: my mother's hours of driving, her conversations with my teachers to make sure they accommodated me at school, her patient explanations of how to interact with people and advocate for myself, her unwavering steadiness against the storms of my teenage years when I could not work out how to exist in the world as a young deaf woman, her gentle hand that touched my shoulder when I buried my good ear into the pillow after a tantrum and refused to speak or listen to anyone.

*

The blue gum has an extensive root system, supporting a trunk that grows firm and tall. In some countries it has been declared a weed because of its vigorous growth and tendency to suck up water.

During storms, when the tree outside the window thrashed in the wind, I asked my father if it would snap.

'No,' he replied. 'It's very strong.'

My father's knowledge of the natural world was broad. Often, as I walked beside him through the paddocks, he would explain the science behind cloud formations, the release of pollen from grasses in spring, or how locust storms could decimate a crop.

Before he met my mother in Sydney, he drove a taxi during the day and took art classes at night. When my parents moved to the farm, my father drove the header, crutched sheep, fed the pigs and mended fences, then painted watercolours in his studio in the evenings. He cut my mother's flowers, arranged them in vases and used them as subjects in his watercolour paintings, a chiaroscuro of colourful blooms and foliage against a black background.

When we moved to the tablelands of Anaiwan country in New England, my father renovated a rambling nineteenth-century house and my mother started a cold-climate garden. She sowed irises and jonquils, a white wisteria that twisted over a blue trellis, three raised vegetable beds and an espaliered apple tree. She tended to her perennials with blood and bone, pulled out weeds, deadheaded roses, watered with a hose in the early morning on hot summer days, and cut the lawn's edges with a pair of scissors before my father bought her an edge trimmer.

*

After I left school, I travelled south-east to the coast, where I began my training as a writer, but I often returned to Armidale for visits. At the beginning of 2015, I attended a conference on contemporary Australian literature and politics at the local university, presenting a paper on literary activism and the decaying Great Barrier Reef. My mother came to collect me at the end of the day's presentations, parking halfway down the hill from the university. I met her as she walked up towards me.

'There were no parks,' she said, puffing. 'I couldn't park any closer. It's annoying.'

I gestured behind me to the lecture theatre. 'It's only a few metres away.'

She shook her head, pulling out her Ventolin inhaler. 'Can't breathe.'

I frowned, waiting for her to catch her breath.

It was the first year of my mother's retirement. She and my father were avid travellers, and that year they expected to go to Asia with my brother. As the trip approached, my mother's apprehension grew. Eventually she conceded, 'It's too difficult. I don't feel well enough.'

We assumed that it was another lung infection, one of many that had occurred throughout her life, and from which she would improve. However, in conversations that year, she repeated that she couldn't breathe. After much cajoling, she agreed to see a specialist, although it meant a visit to Sydney. The specialist checked her into a hospital to have her lungs cleaned out.

My mother came home feeling better, but when the results of the specialist's examination came through a few weeks later, we discovered her diagnosis was more severe than we had imagined. It was bronchiectasis, a condition in which the bronchi (those branches) are permanently enlarged after a period of inflammation. In a standard pair of lungs, the bronchi are coated with mucus to protect them from particles moving into the airways, but with bronchiectasis, the widened bronchi gather much more mucus, making them vulnerable to infection, and thus repeating the cycle. In my mother's case, a bacteria called pseudomonas was the cause of her infections. It had been living in the bottom of her lungs for so long that it was impossible to treat. The only thing the doctor could do was put her on antibiotics to suppress it, although it continued to flare up, leaving her constantly short of breath.

The trajectory of my mother's illness was clear: the infections would continue, her lungs would deteriorate, and she likely only had a few years left to live.

*

In her 2015 essay 'The Forest at the Edge of Time', Ashley Hay references research that indicates that gum trees, if left to their own devices, have quite a narrow geographical range. With temperatures rapidly increasing due to climate change, eucalypts – which, like other trees, 'tend to be one of the least nimble of organisms in terms of their capacity to adapt to a shift in something like climate' – will be badly affected.[1] Not only are temperatures a problem; so too are the bushfires of the twenty-first century.

By the time bushfires broke out near Armidale in early September 2019, the town was on Level Five water restrictions due to the endless drought. Each person was limited to 160 litres per day, and my mother skipped showers to save her irises. The town, which was used to foggy days in winter, was now shrouded in smoke.

The machines that cleared the air were caught up in the inferno. A mature tree can manufacture enough oxygen for ten people for a year. Brett Summerall, Director of Research and Chief Botanist at Sydney's Royal Botanic Gardens, indicated in an interview with Georgina Reid, editor of *The Planthunter*, that between three and seven billion trees were burnt. The loss of oxygen production from these trees is staggering. Yet it wasn't just trees. Up to 19 million hectares were burnt, consisting of, as Reid writes, 'shrubs, climbers, groundcover, fungi, moss: the microscopic and the magnificent'.[2]

Scientists don't know how long it will take the forests and shrubs to recover, but what is clear is that with more frequent events like these, they simply won't be able to catch their breath.

*

I visited my parents in November 2019, before flying to Munich to take up my fellowship. The smoky air stuck at the back of my throat when I breathed. My mother couldn't go outside because of her lungs. For someone whose daily joy was planting, pruning, weeding, digging, transplanting, mulching and watering, to stay inside was a punishment.

From the cold and snow of Munich, I watched the infernos on the news. On the last day of 2019, my mother emailed, 'Bloody hot – 34 today 36 by end of week. No rain, smoke and dust.' Nearly a fortnight later she wrote, 'Little bit of rain in a storm here so it hasn't forgotten how.' Four weeks after that she added, 'We have had lovely rain here at last which has lifted spirits. Things I thought were gone in the garden have popped up albeit a little later so that is most encouraging.'

While the rain began to restore her garden, the broader damage was unfathomable. Nearly three billion animals, and sixty billion invertebrates, were killed or displaced by the loss of plants and trees. Many people, such as Vanessa Cavanagh, who has Bundjalung and Wonnarua heritage, lost more than trees. Writing in *The Conversation*, Cavanagh explains the death of a grandmother tree in Colo Heights, on the edge of Darkinjung country, as 'a deep hurt of losing someone far older and wiser than me. Losing someone who was respected and adored. Someone with knowledge I cannot fathom or comprehend.'[3] It was the loss of kin.

*

After the frightening journey from Munich to my parents' house on the coast, I was relieved to be safe. As I couldn't get across the border to see Bruce in Queensland, I waited for six weeks for my parents to arrive for their winter stay. By the time we reunited, my mother was desperate for a fresh face – she hadn't seen anyone other than my father for three months. It went without saying that if my mother caught Covid-19 at that point, she wouldn't survive.

The house on the coast sat in a quiet cul-de-sac. Visited by bush turkeys by day and cane toads by night, I continued working on my research and writing, collaborating with my colleagues in Munich via Zoom. My movements were contained to the local beach, the grocery store and a nearby café. I washed my hands vigorously each time I returned to the house, anxious about infecting my mother.

Covid-19 attacks the cells in the lungs' alveoli, causing them to leak fluid. The air sacs become clogged and inflamed, affecting the lungs' capacity to take in air. Patients who decline may be given the same apparatuses that my mother used: nasal cannulas and CPAP machines, the industrial equivalents of trees.

A few years and permutations later, she caught the virus from my father. For a tense couple of days, we waited; the vaccinations meant she pulled through. My father, also vaccinated, coughed for weeks.

*

I didn't inherit my mother's green thumb, preferring to lie under a fan with a book than dig my fingers into the soil. But as she continued to deteriorate, it seemed important to me that I try to carry out what I had learned from watching her in the garden. In the thin rim of dirt surrounding my subtropical, inner-city patio, the yuccas and the tulipwood tree looked after themselves, but the other plants looked dejected. I tried to remember to water my pots of bird's nest ferns and bromeliads. Large green caterpillars chewed through half of the monstera's thick leaves. I sprayed them and Bruce told me off for poisoning the ecosystem. I overwatered the grevillea, and it turned brown and died.

I tried harder. I fed my Madonna lily for the first time in years and it suddenly had enough nutrients to flower. I noticed that pieces of the jade plant, knocked over in a storm, had regenerated in a neighbouring pot. A golden orb spider built its web between the two yuccas. Putting my linen in the washing machine one morning, I saw a blue-tongued lizard trundling past the laundry door. It seemed that I might be able, however haphazardly, to continue my mother's lifelong practice of care.

*

I teach my students, particularly those with disabilities, not to be shy, but to advocate for themselves – just as my parents taught me. I also teach them, as my mother taught me, to never use the words 'got' or 'a lot'. ('There's always a better word,' I explain, as she used to do.) I listen to them carefully, as my mother did when friends visited with their problems. One student, grappling with a story about a river red gum, tells me that he can't get away from the human-centredness of the story.

'Think like a tree,' I suggest.

He sends me another draft. In his opening, he describes the life of a seed that has fallen from the gum, recounting its growth and witnessing of the world. While the story needs work, I am drawn to the beginning, to the seed and its old parent. Amidst the persistent sorrow of my mother's impending death, it was a sliver of silvery light.

*

As the years passed, I watched my mother struggling to garden. She often sat on the wooden edge of the raised vegetable bed to catch her breath. We never talked about what was happening but, as someone who was restricted by a disability, I sensed how frustrated she was.

Eventually, she couldn't live without the oxygen at all. Her legs swelled because her heart didn't have enough power for circulation. Her world dwindled to the bedroom, the bathroom, the kitchen table and the television. She was unsteady on her feet and fell a few times, once ending up in hospital, where she was lonely and bored. I was coming for a visit I had booked a few months before. Determined to leave the hospital before I arrived, she refused to take her medication.

'What are you doing, Mum?' we exclaimed.

'If I don't take the meds, the doctor has to come and see me, and then I can make sure he signs off on my discharge.'

The next day she texted us, triumphant, 'I got out!'

After another fall, the thin skin of her legs split open. My mother finally accepted palliative care, and nurses appeared, gentle and humorous.

They changed the dressings on her legs every two days and carefully explained the options for end-of-life care. Their kindness reminded me of the mycelium in tree roots, connecting the community out of sight.

Soon my mother was confined to the couch, to a chair, then to a bed that my father and brother erected before the windows, where she looked out at the garden she had tended for twenty years.

Friends began to say their goodbyes. My mother shared with me an email which a fellow book lover had sent: *I know you are the 'light' in all of James' paintings and whenever I see that wonderful yellow light I shall think of you.*

*

In his poem 'A Valediction: Forbidding Mourning', John Donne opens with the image of a group of mournful friends gathered around the bedsides of 'virtuous men' who 'whisper to their souls to go'. Some of these friends, observing carefully, say, 'The breath goes now.'

This poem frequently came to mind as my mother's life drew to a close. It was hard for me to loosen our bonds, woven so tightly through our car trips and conversations, the constant contrapuntal of my anxieties and her reassurances.

One morning I emerged into the kitchen, having woken unusually early. My mother was already there; even as she became sicker and sicker, she still woke up at 6.30am and sat at the table with a cup of tea.

'You and I,' she said quietly, 'we're real soulmates.'

I dissolved into a flood of tears. 'I don't know what I'll do when you're gone.'

'You'll be unsettled for a while, but you'll be alright,' my mother insisted. 'You will.'

Donne ends his first stanza with the words 'The breath goes now, and some say, no.' My mother's absence was never written in the pages of my life; the thought of it was inconceivable to me. But as I watched her sipping air to stay alive, I knew that it was time for her to go.

*

For months I flew back and forth to the tablelands. I slept badly and lost weight. Each time I would return because we thought the end was near, then my mother would rally and I'd fly back for work.

We talked about euthanasia. It would be at least another six weeks before she could access the drugs, due to the checks and balances, but she was in chronic pain and her brain, usually sharp and incisive, began to dull from a lack of oxygen. I sensed that she was having difficulty deciding what to do.

'Mum, you don't have to do euthanasia if you don't want to. We can get more time off from work. I don't want you to feel pressured.'

She shook her head. 'I'm fucking up everyone's life. Your father's exhausted. I look at the roses in the garden and I can't move. I'm in agony.'

I wanted to tell her that I would have done anything to keep her on earth, but I didn't want to add to her distress.

*

I packed up my suitcase again and booked another flight from Armidale to Adelaide. I needed to return to work for a week to run some symposiums for graduate students and researchers.

'Don't die while I'm away,' I said, half-joking, as I hugged her after another trip. Her body was small and frail, her shoulders bony.

I hardly unpacked my suitcase. I ran the first symposium, then swam at the pool down the road, crying into my goggles, the world blurring. The rhythm of stroking laps calmed me, and when I climbed out of the pool I snapped a photo of the water and nearby spotted gums and put it on my Facebook page. 'Looks lovely and peaceful,' my mother commented. Busy with work, I didn't comment in return.

We thought we had a few weeks left, but on the day I ran the second symposium, my mother started to decline, complaining of pain in her feet and her stomach. My brother texted me, concerned, but I couldn't get a ticket until the next morning, with a three-hour layover in Sydney. At the airport café in Sydney I drank several coffees and tried to read a student's work. My brother was worried that my sister and I wouldn't make it in time.

For the first time ever, my Qantas flight arrived early.

My brother, waiting at home with our mother, said to her, 'Dad has just gone to the airport to get Jess.' She was heavily sedated with morphine and hunched over, desperate for breath.

'I have to go,' she told him, but he didn't understand what she was saying, thinking that she needed the bathroom.

When I arrived, he explained to her loudly, 'Jess is here.' I held her hand. Her face, which had always brightened when I entered a room, remained blank. My brother's eyes were red with tears. I couldn't bear it and turned away to make him a coffee.

Ten minutes later, having held on for as long as she could, she exhaled for the last time.

*

In the short cosmic horror film *The Sky*, directed by Matt Sears, two young women sit on a grassy hill in fold-out chairs, backpacks and a picnic rug at their feet. In the distance, above green fields divided by hedgerows, colossal black clouds gather, striped with lightning. The girls, drinking from plastic cups of rosé and chewing magic mushrooms, play a game of 'Never Have I Ever'. Glancing at the horizon, one of them says quietly, 'Never have I ever been so scared.'

A little while later, this woman receives a voicemail message from her mother, apologising for their difficult relationship. It transpires that her friend has tricked her into spending their last few hours together. The girl, her sense of reality distorted by drugs, rushes away from the knoll and through the forest in fear and agitation. When she finally reaches her mother, the apocalypse hits, and her mother's face peels into nothingness.

*

I read the work of fellow authors who write about Australia's natural world, about Country. Some of them dwell on losing their parents, the way it opens their selves up to the wider losses of extinction, melting ice, dwindling migrations. James Bradley, in 'An Ocean and an Instant', weaves an account of his father's decline and death with the loss of the insects in his childhood in Glenelg, on Kaurna country, and the attempted extinction of Kaurna people. Dwelling on the statistics of species loss (which in Australia is knitted with the murder and dispossession of First Nations peoples), he comments, 'The scale of the convulsion taking place around us is almost unimaginable.'[4]

I find, harbouring loss in my body, that the other losses around the globe – of ice, of humans and animals in the wars in Palestine and Ukraine, of species that disappear before we become properly familiar with them – bear down on me like rockfall.

*

My mother wanted her body to go to the university for science, but because of the wounds in her legs, the people at the university explained, her skin was not intact and she couldn't be embalmed. Her next option was to be burned to ash and dusted across her favourite rose garden.

The day we decided to scatter her ashes, a storm was tracking in orange across the Bureau of Meteorology's online rain radar. We figured we had about ninety minutes before it hit. At the garden, large clouds bloomed against a slate-grey sky. We dug into the box of gritty ash with our hands and threw it against the beds of pink, white, red, yellow and orange roses. The clouds, pushing closer, took on a green sheen which meant they were holding hail.

The first drops slapped our skin as we washed our hands at the tap. Looking at the roiling clouds, we hastened to the car. The storm slammed down as my father drove slowly along the road. We were cocooned in a world of white hail, a newly configured family of four. Behind us the rain pounded my mother's body into the earth, food for slaters, earthworms and, perhaps one day, a eucalyptus seed.

Safety Jumps

It was a six-hour drive from the hot, dry plains of Boggabri, in Gamilaroi country, to the beaches of Sydney. My father, who rarely stopped to let us out for the toilet or to stretch our legs, was once booked for speeding. We stayed at Roseville with Dad's childhood friend, Wendy, and her family. Wendy, who had lived not far from my father as he grew up and who attended the same school as my sister and me in Armidale, became close to my mother. Later, another friend of Wendy's introduced me to her daughter, Jo, who studied creative writing with me at Wollongong and in turn became my good friend.

Sometimes we met the family on the Central Coast, once camping at Pretty Beach where cicadas massed in the trees. Their mating calls, thrumming through their bodies, were so loud that they hurt my ear. Down by the beach, I never ventured into the ocean on my own, but always waited for my brother.

I was used to contained bodies of water. Dad had installed an above-ground pool when I was six or seven, erecting a flagpole next to it for whimsy. My brother changed the flag most mornings. His favourite was the white skull and crossbones on a black background (he was obsessed with pirates at the time). It was so hot in the summers that as soon as we arrived home from school we stepped into our swimmers, stood on the upturned fertiliser bucket next to the pool's rim, and clambered into the water. We chased each other around the circular edge of the pool until we made a whirlpool, then floated in the vortex. At other times I exhaled a trail of silvery bubbles and sat, cross-legged, on the plastic floor, my long hair streaming around me.

In my early twenties, I described this state of suspension in a short story which we workshopped in a creative writing class in America, where I was on exchange. My teacher, Clark Blaise, commented, 'Isn't this a great metaphor for the author, with ideas streaming from their head like hair?'

I blinked. I hadn't intended for the young girl to represent a writer, but perhaps I had depicted the way my imagination unfurled and loosened whenever I dived and swam in water.

The other place where we swam in summer was Dripping Rock. My father and his two brothers threw the kids into the back of a ute and drove east from the farm. The gravel road became potholed and corrugated, and our father's tools rattled in the ute tray alongside us. We passed the pyromaniac who would come to burn down his own house and, later, one brother and his wife's house after they left the farm. Halfway up the hill we parked the ute, and our mothers and grandparents pulled up behind us in cars. We unpacked picnic baskets and billy cans and then, in single file, skipped over stones and trickles of water and ducked under the low boughs of trees until we came to the clearing with the tall shelf of rock.

Even if it was a baking day, the temperature of the pool of water was cold, being overshadowed by the stretch of rock. I waited for my older cousins to wade in first, then followed, the water biting. I swam as fast as I could to the other side of the pool, where there was a shallow cave in the rock. I had to swim fast otherwise leeches would latch onto my leg.

*

A few years later, Dad installed a larger pool in our backyard. In place of the fertiliser bucket he built steps and a deck, from which we dive-bombed into the water. The kelpie ran up the steps too, barking when we splashed water at her. If my brother, sister and I weren't swimming in our pool, we were at our cousins' pools. One family had a yellow plastic blow-up horse with black stripes, but I could never stay on it. Meningitis had ruined not just my hearing but also my balance.

An adult or a cousin was always nearby, and I ran to them if there was trouble (such as the time I threw the chlorine dispenser, nicknamed Alfie, at my brother in a fit of rage and hit him on the head, creating a shocking and sudden amount of blood). Swimming was usually safe.

*

The sea was a different story. Family films from the '80s show a round-tummied and knock-kneed two-year-old Jessica tottering across the sand while her sister and cousins belted past. When I was five and six, and Christmas was over, and Dad and his two brothers had finally finished the harvest, I itched for the hot crunch of sand beneath my soles and foam nibbling my skin.

Once in the ocean, though, I never swam far. My father explained repeatedly about rips and I was fearful of getting stuck in one. The sea could carry me out beyond the breakers where, I was sure,

Mrs Woodley's swim safety lessons would not save me. I was also sure that each time a leathery piece of kelp grazed my skin, it was a shark.

On one holiday, when I was ten, I surfaced from a dive and saw people making for the shore. A lifeguard was shouting into a megaphone, but I couldn't make out the words. I looked around for my brother, who was wading towards me. 'There's a shark, Jess! You have to get out of the water.' We swam furiously through the waves, my breath sharp and shallow. When I felt gritty sand beneath my feet and sloughed out of the water, I wondered: *What if my brother hadn't been there?*

Deafness and sharks, even though their attacks are rare, are some of the reasons I tend not to take physical risks. I map out a walking route to work that has minimal traffic, swim in enclosed spaces such as pools, rarely run in the dark, and never walk in the bush without a companion. These decisions are based on my knowledge that if I call out for help, I will not be able to hear an answer, nor will I be able to hear someone or something about to attack me.

*

By the end of 2020, I had become increasingly restless in Brisbane because I could not thrive in my role, which was not secure anyway. In 2021 I moved from the humid, sticky atmosphere of the subtropics to the dry air of Kaurna country in Adelaide. I had only visited the city once before, on a stopover on the Indian Pacific when I made my first trip to Noongar country in Western Australia. We had five hours to kill, so I hopped into a taxi with some other passengers from the train and headed into the city. I spent forty-five minutes in the Art Gallery of South Australia, pausing before a Tom Roberts, then the gallery closed.

I walked to McDonalds, had a burger and chips at a plastic table, then caught a taxi back to the train.

This time, I started my new job at a university and rented a brick cottage. The houses, the dry air and the regular layout of the city made me feel like I was back in regional New South Wales. I formed a routine, stopping for a coffee in the mornings at a café whose staff beamed when I opened the door, then walking through the back of the campus to my office. If it had rained, the smell of the lemon-scented gums, *Corymbia citriodora*, perfumed the air. When I breathed it in, my pulse settled. The same gums had grown on the farm.

A 50-metre pool is just down the road from my house. It is a simple municipal pool of six lanes, open for six months of the year. Spotted gums hang over the water and drop in their leaves and twigs. Sometimes, plunging through the pool, I will surface with a gum leaf stuck to my cheek. At quiet times, attendants stroke a long-handled net over the surface, scooping out the leaves.

I try to time my visits when it's less busy, usually mid-morning or mid-afternoon, because sharing lanes makes it hard for me to meditate. Large men, in particular, don't have a sense of the contours of their body. They manspread in the lane, displacing water and my thoughts.

Normally I take my writing problems into the water, such as a story in which the next plot step is opaque to me, or an argument for an essay that won't knit together. I hold the knots in my mind and, usually, after half an hour of laps, I untangle them and pick up the thread of my narrative again.

After my mother's death, I swam to keep myself from unravelling. The point of exercise, my psychologist told me, light pouring through the window into her room, was to burn off the adrenaline that kept my mind racing at night, shutting out sleep.

I examined my old Speedos. My body had changed shape since my previous spurt of swimming, and they no longer fit. On reading how Olympic swimmers are more likely to get melanomas from the hours beneath the Australian sun, I bought a suit that covered my back, leaving just my legs, arms and face to smear in sunscreen.

I churned up and down the lane, my stomach spasming with tears. Muscle built on my shoulders and arms, making it easier to lift my suitcase when I made trips back inland to visit my father.

*

Roger Deakin inaugurated the wild swimming genre with *Waterlog*,[1] in which he recounts his journey of following the rain and swimming through the British Isles to the sea. In this book's wake drifted Jessica Lee's *Turning*.[2] To get over a period of sadness after a break-up, Lee sets herself the task of swimming in a different lake in Germany every week, even in winter. Later, in *Small Bodies of Water*,[3] Nina Mingya Powles describes in rich, compressed prose her relationships with pools and the sea in Hong Kong, Aotearoa and London. Ingrid Horrocks, in *Where We Swim*,[4] depicts the waterways of Aotearoa, many of which are so polluted they are unsafe for swimming.

I would like to swim as these writers do, in ponds, lakes and rivers, but I could never do it on my own. In some places, where the water isn't fresh, I risk infecting my only working ear again. Besides, where Deakin describes lap swimming as 'the frustration of a lifetime doing lengths, of endlessly turning back on myself like a tiger pacing its cage',[5] I find comfort in the rhythm of lap swimming and of knowing where the bodies in a pool are positioned. If I can see them, I won't run into them and risk an awkward conversation. And, like a poem with rules for syllables and rhyme, the laps create structure. My mind, as I pull through the water, floats free.

As I read these books, however, a question gnaws at me: where are the memoirs of deaf writers and the water?

*

Cindy-Lu Bailey, profoundly deaf since birth, trained at the Cabramatta Swimming Club. At age twelve, she won her first medal, a bronze at the 1977 Deaflympics. In 1982, when she was seventeen, she represented the national team in the Commonwealth Games.

In an interview following a race, she was asked, 'With your deafness, how do you know when the starter's gun goes off?'

She replied, 'I feel the vibrations from the gun, and sometimes when I can't hear, I follow the other girls that go off.'

Later, in an interview with Auslan interpreter Tony Clews, she explained that she'd had an advantage because of her deafness: she was allowed up to three false starts. She would watch the calves of the swimmer to her right. As their muscles tightened, Cindy-Lu knew they were about to dive, and this was her cue to dive too. Once her competitors had worked this out, they tensed their muscles deliberately to unsettle her. Unsurprisingly, she found the Deaflympics friendlier to compete in.[6]

Deaf and hard of hearing swimmers now have strobe lights on the starter blocks. Some hearing swimmers choose to respond to these because light travels faster than sound.

*

After my eardrum ruptured, leaving me almost completely deaf for weeks, I took more care with my right ear. When I swam, I plugged it up with silicone.

In the water I heard nothing at all, and relied on vision to work out what was happening around me. If someone asked me to move out of a lane when they were training, I never heard them. Once, I only realised I had to get out when a row of muscular bodies barrelled towards me. If I'm sharing a lane and need to pause at the end to let the other person swim ahead, I can usually lip-read them, but because I can't hear my voice, the pitch is never loud enough for them to hear my replies. I just smile and turn into another lap.

Without sound, I focus on the patterns of light on the water, trying to stay left of the black line and occasionally running into the plastic lane markers. The tang of chlorine marks my skin. I can also smell the deodorant of the man who gets into the water without showering first.

*

My mother had been a fantastic swimmer when she was young. Black-and-white photos show her with medals strung around her neck.

I write to one of her childhood friends in Aotearoa, asking for more information about my mother's swimming. Mum won the Monica Thacker competition for lifesaving, her friend writes. 'She was a lovely swimmer. I don't recall her as speedy but she did amazingly well with the lifesaving team.' She trained a cohort of swimmers, which included this friend. At the examination Mum's friend was, she added, 'terrified I would fail and let her down, but we made the grade and she, as with everything, was successful'.

I smile, on reading this, to find my mother's characteristics already manifesting: a complete faith in one's ability, combined with an intimidating demeanour that meant you were anxious about disappointing her. Failing was never an option.

*

My mother stopped swimming later in life because she was concerned about ruining her hair. She used to say, 'Jessica is the only one of us that can swim.'

At Boggabri Primary School, the weeks leading up to Christmas were so full of heat, the children so ratty and restless and distracted, that the teachers gave up on teaching and set craft activities instead. I plastered a balloon with strips of newspaper and glue, attached four cups torn from egg cartons on the bottom and one on the side, then painted it yellow. When the yellow coating dried, I painted eyes above the one cup on the side so that it became a pig with a snout. Another time we made clay coil pots and painted them with glaze and our teacher took them away to be fired. Mine returned coated in the colour of diarrhoea. Mum still kept her loose coins and safety pins in it.

The last week or two was intensive swimming, which began in the morning before the heat became too strong. We lined up beneath the jacaranda trees, flowering with a profusion of purple, then walked through the school gate and wide tarmac roads to the pool. The sun was already eating the backs of our necks.

Having spent most of our childhoods in the pool, our final years at school were largely swimming laps, with a few swim safety lessons. Mrs Woodley, long arms outstretched and leg out to the front, demonstrated a safety jump. 'If a ship is going down, you need to jump into the water like this.'

We practised jumping off the hot concrete rim of the pool, arms out, legs making triangles.

Later, I asked Mrs Woodley, 'Why can't you wait until the ship sinks lower into the water and then jump? Then you don't have to leap from so high.'

'Because it's dangerous.'

'But why?'

She didn't give me an answer. The question bothered me for years, until I worked out that the drag of the sinking ship would pull me down with it, so it was best to jump from a great height to clear the drag.

On Fridays, Mum gave us twenty cents to buy a bag of sweets from the pool's canteen. On carnival days we could buy a Buffalo Bill icecream, chewing on the bubblegum until our tongues were blue.

*

Like my mother, I was never good enough to win medals, but I was persistent. At my school in Armidale, I decided to try for the Bronze Medallion, an award one needed before becoming a qualified life saver. Wearing my swimmers beneath denim jeans and my father's flannel shirt, I thrashed from one end of the pool to the other to prove that I could swim if I was thrown overboard, fully clothed. The point of keeping one's clothes on, I was told, was to prevent hypothermia.

When I hauled myself out, water rushed from the jeans. The flannel shirt stuck to my skin, cold and clammy. I also practised bringing my brother into an imaginary shore, cupping his chin and tugging him along with a lopsided sidestroke. Somehow I passed the examination and received a medallion the size of a coin.

I have never had formal swimming training. It's too difficult to organise, what with having to stop up my hearing ear with silicon. I'd have to keep taking the silicone out to listen to an instructor.

'Watch some YouTube videos,' Bruce suggested.

I connected my hearing aid to my laptop with Bluetooth and watched swimmers on YouTube. In the pool, I practised breathing on my left ear after every third stroke, instead of always breathing on the right, as Mrs Woodley taught us to do. Water kept slipping into my mouth. I thought of my mother, snatching at air.

*

In *Swimming Studies*, Canadian writer and artist Leanne Shapton, who trained to be an Olympic swimmer, explains the difference between swimming short course in Canada (25 metres) and swimming long course (50 metres). Describing a swimming meet, she writes, 'Swimming long course again feels luxurious, Californian. An outdoor fifty-meter expanse of water shimmers with the same kind of American dream that football fields and baseball diamonds do.'[7] It dawns on me that there are more indoor pools in Canada because of the cold. In Australia, with its light, heat and space, 50-metre pools are the norm.

The pool down the road in Adelaide shuts for winter a couple of weeks after Easter. This year it was balmy enough to swim in late April. Out in the street, the European trees were quietly turning. The light was long and low, with only a handful of swimmers in the lanes. After twenty-four laps I finished, watching the trees' shadows falling into the pool, feeling the stillness of the air.

*

I did not heed my teacher's lesson to jump before the ship went down. I was dragged into the dark undertow, the sea pouring out through my eyes.

I wrote to my friend Jo, who Wendy had introduced me to at her house in Roseville, before we started our creative writing degrees at the University of Wollongong. Jo lost her father a few months before Mum died, and she was also exhausted. She thought it was because life did not stop. One still had to work and cook dinner.

I was reminded of the lethargy of my days in London, when the lack of abundant light cast me down. I had not wanted to take antidepressants, fearful that I wouldn't be able to write my PhD thesis. This time around, I was so far down underwater that I was willing to try anything.

In the doctor's surgery, still crying, I obtained a prescription for antidepressants and a medical certificate. I flew back to Brisbane and lay on Bruce's bed for a week, staring at the dust that had accumulated on the fan blades.

'Don't you want to do something about the fan?' I asked him.

'Why?'

'Because I have to look at it.'

He grinned. The dust was going nowhere.

*

Every few days I headed to the pool at Musgrave Park. In 2017 I swam there for Swim for the Reef, a fundraiser for the Environmental Defenders Office. I joined Team Avid, run by my local bookstore, Avid Reader. The bookstore's owner, Fiona, and some local writers were among us. Fiona brought watermelons soaked in lime juice, which we ate on the stands, while a green ant climbed into my friend Anita's shoe and bit her three times, before migrating to my foot.

I had trained for months, and although I was not a fast swimmer, I was steady, swimming several kilometres without stopping. When, in one race, it looked like I was going to beat local writer Steve of the Wobbegongs, he grabbed my ankle and pulled me back.

'I was winning!' I sputtered when we reached the blocks. 'And you stopped me!'

Steve tried to look chastened.

The pool has been upgraded since then, the murals of jellyfish on the pool floor covered with pale-blue paint. The water was heated, and with winter sun falling onto my back as I stroked out laps, I was cocooned.

*

The medication stripped me of all grief, anxiety, ambition, sadness, drive and desire. My tears dried up and physical energy poured through my muscles. Watching the fan turn with its load of dust, I realised how much emotional stress my body harboured, and why I was chronically exhausted.

As I feared, I could not write, and I had deadlines. After a few weeks I threw the packet of tablets in the bin. They had worked well enough to get me back to Adelaide and to my desk, at least.

Back on Kaurna country, it was still winter, so I headed to the 25-metre indoor pool at work. I lost track of my laps because the pool was so short. Light fell through the windows into the water, patterning the pool floor. On rainy days water rushed down the windows in arcs. I missed the spotted gums.

Quintessence

While waiting for the jug to boil, Bruce stood before the glass sliding doors to the brick patio, watching a golden orb-weaver spider that had built its home in the fronds of my bird's nest fern. In a former life, when he was an ecologist, his favourite part of the job was going into the paddocks and bush to check for bugs and animals, as well as vegetation type and quality, when assessing claims for environmental offsets. It was rare to see him so focused on something other than a computer screen.

I joined him at the glass door and asked, 'What is it about the spider?'

'She's cleaning her web.'

'How do you know it's a female?'

'Because of her size. There's the male.'

I followed his finger, squinting, and found a small, grey spider, about a fifth of the female's size, sitting near the edge of the web.

'You can tell from her abdomen that she's going to have babies.'

The kettle clicked off and Bruce turned away to make his coffee.

I continued to observe the spider. The neat rows of her eyes made me feel cross-eyed, and when her delicate legs, striped with black and yellow, reached across the web, my skin tightened. I imagined the babies, when born, streaming from their egg sac like a soft, grey wave.

*

In Franz Kafka's iconic story 'The Metamorphosis', Gregor Samsa wakes up one morning and finds he has been turned into a huge insect. His back is hard, as though 'armour-plated', and he discovers a 'dome-like brown belly divided into stiff arched segments'. His voice changes into something that is 'no human voice'. On seeing his transformation, his mother faints, his father bursts into tears, and his employer, upon visiting the house to see why Gregor isn't at work, backs away in horror. Although Gregor's sister initially attempts to accommodate him with food, as the family's circumstances become more difficult without their breadwinner, their distaste increases. Eventually, his sister declares, 'We must get rid of it.' Gregor, listless and depressed, starves to death. His corpse is disposed of by the cleaning lady.[1]

I first read this tale at age fourteen, entranced by its conceit of a man living as an insect. Re-reading it thirty years later, I see past the clever literary mechanism to read it as negotiating something that has afflicted me and many other disabled people: an inability to care for us because we are unlike nondisabled people.

*

The golden orb-weaver is named for its web, which has a golden sheen. The colour is thought to attract insects – such as flies, mosquitoes, grasshoppers, cicadas – and sometimes even small birds. Its web looks like a cross-section of a tree trunk, with spikes radiating from a core (often placed towards the top of the web) and fine parallel threads encircling the core like growth rings. The web is encircled by a frame of stiff threads that connects it to supports such as trees, fences or wires. When an insect hits the web, the threads capturing it can stretch to 2.7 times their original length as they absorb the insect's energy.[2]

In 2015 and 2016, a team of researchers from the University of the Sunshine Coast, led by Genevieve Kerr, collected silk from two species of golden orbs, *Nephila pilipes* and *Nephila plumipes*. They moved within a 10-kilometre radius of Buderim in Queensland, gathering pieces of webs from subtropical rainforests, backyards, planted forests and farmland. The researchers took bundles of silk fibre from the frame of each web, because spiders often reinforce this section with multiple threads. Previous studies had also focused on the radial threads, which have fewer fibres. Using a stress-testing machine, the researchers found that the silk is up to one hundred times tougher than the synthetic thread used in medical surgeries. It has the capacity to be used for sutures and stents, and for making motorcycle riding or bullet-proof clothing. It can't be farmed like the silk of silkworms, however, because the spiders would eat one another.[3]

*

Over the five years that I lived with Bruce in the house with the golden orb and bird's nest fern, we made a home with bookcases, velvet couches and his mother's and my father's paintings. The mock orange by the fence perfumed the air powerfully in spring, and on still winter nights I could sometimes hear the call of curlews by the river. We argued over whose turn it was to get the coffee in the mornings, drank too much shiraz on Friday nights and shouted about feminism, watched B-grade movies and cat videos, and talked about Maria Sibylla Merian, a seventeenth-century German naturalist and entomologist, and Phillipa Foot, a twentieth-century philosopher. He kept me awake at night with his restless leg; I woke him up with snoring and talking in my sleep. I complained that he didn't notice the grease in the kitchen, but laughed when he replied, 'Are you clutching your pearls?' One night, out with a friend, he didn't come home until 5am, by which stage I had called the police to find out if he was in the cells or the local hospital.

I was often away, travelling for conferences, residencies, research or book events. Each time it was like pulling a branch from a tree, the slow sap of soreness welling up. I ignored it by concentrating on my writing and work.

*

In 2012, the Victoria and Albert Museum in London unveiled a richly yellow cape and shawl made from the silk of Madagascan female spiders. The project was prompted by Nicholas Godley and Simon Peers, a Briton and American who had lived in Madagascar for several years. Every morning, sixty to eighty people ventured in and around the capital of Madagascar, Antananarivo, to look for spiders. The arachnids were brought to a 'spidery', where they were harnessed to a hand-operated machine developed by Godley and Peers from a design illustrated more than a century ago. Twenty-four spiders were placed in a group and milked (or 'silked' as it was called) for twenty-five minutes, then returned to the wild.

The group of workers created a twenty-four-strand thread. These threads were bound into thicker threads and used to weave a shawl via traditional weaving methods from the Madagascan highlands. The shawl was brocaded with geometric shapes representing birds and flowers. The threads were also used to create a cape of taffeta, onto which motifs of the golden orb were embroidered.

On YouTube, I watched the Madagascan weavers at work. They wore white coats and leaned on white sheets of paper to protect the fabric, their careful fingers quick and precise, their eyes intent.[4] Peers describes how, the first time he touched the spider silk, he couldn't believe how soft and light it was.[5] This is due to the structure of the silk, which is round, while the structure of silkworm silk is more irregular. He can barely feel the garment on his skin, and yet the thread is so strong.

The robe is undeniably gorgeous, but I was disturbed by the extractivism of the project: it involved 1.2 million spiders and three years of labour from hands that collected, spun, wove, embroidered and sewed. All for an object that sits behind glass.

*

Five years ago, I left the house with the bird's nest fern and the golden orb spider to take up a permanent academic job in Adelaide. As I packed, I was not entirely sure that I had made the right decision. I only knew that I could no longer thrive in the place where I was, surviving on part-time work and contracts. I needed the security of a job so that I could write and research well.

'What will you do if I go?' I asked Bruce.

'Don't stay in Brisbane to look after me,' he said gently.

I found a new place to live, moved in one of the velvet couches and some of our paintings, and bought new furniture. As on other occasions, I cauterised my sadness by immersing myself in work. We tried to maintain our relationship through Skype, but neither of us are big talkers. I flew to Brisbane, worrying about carbon emissions. I spoke to a friend about my guilt about leaving Bruce to move interstate. She recommended that we cook dinner and read – the activities we used to do in Brisbane – but via Skype. Bruce and I agreed that watching one another cook was creepy, and when he took out a book on Skype and started turning the pages, I couldn't stop laughing.

I resigned myself to infrequent visits and conversations. When I complained that I was making most of the effort by flying to Brisbane, Bruce blinked at me implacably and continued clipping his toenails. I was annoyed at the time, but later his response made me smile: it was the quintessence of him.

*

When Gregor Samsa turns into an insect, he can no longer care for his sister and parents. He had previously worked in a job he despised to pay for the nice apartment in which they lived, and he was saving to send his sister to a music school. It soon transpires that the family don't need Gregor's income after all, as they have just enough from a nest egg, as well as pay from the menial jobs they find, to support themselves, although their lives are poor.

Where Gregor took his caring responsibilities seriously, his family responds with neglect. His father throws an apple at his son; it lodges in Gregor's back and begins to rot. They do not recognise that Gregor is still largely the same person, although his abilities have changed: he can no longer dress himself, but he is adept at running on the ceiling. His sister, before she becomes indifferent, recognises that the furniture was in the way of Gregor's rambles and begins moving it out. However, Gregor is distressed by the removal of the paintings, for he still loves art.

Reading this story, I see a family so disgusted by disability that they refuse to make the effort to see if their son is still there. Gregor and the reader are left to wonder if they ever cared at all.

One of my university lecturers once mentioned that Gregor's demise, and his removal by the cleaning lady, was a metaphor for the genocide of Jewish people during World War II. The precursor to the gas chambers was the Aktion T4 policy, which entailed the sterilisation and mass extermination of disabled people in Germany, who were seen to be defective.

*

Bruce's fascination with the golden orb stayed with me for years afterwards. Recently, I asked him again, 'What was it about that spider?'

He answered, 'The world is full of rules, spoken and unspoken, and I'm trying to work out what they are.'

Over our decade-long relationship I have come to understand that Bruce finds it hard to read faces and emotions, just as I find it hard to hear. We both get tired from trying to put the pieces together during social interactions. Where I rely on body language to get by, he looks for patterns and structures.

I wonder if my deafness predisposed me to him. When you are unusual, at least compared to nondisabled people, the world takes on a unique sheen, and I have long found ordinary people dull. I love my partner's sharp intelligence and relentless curiosity, the way his attitudes to relationships vary so much from mine. Like me, he is an observer, watching and working out how to fit in. Perhaps we are both some kind of insect.

*

While golden orb populations are not under threat, insects in general are. A 2017 study of sixty-three protected areas in Germany over nearly thirty years found a more than 75 per cent decline in flying insect biomass.[6] In Australia, bogong moth populations have plummeted. *The Guardian* reports that in 2019, after decades of gradual decline, the numbers dropped catastrophically. Mountain caves that were once thick with moths now have so few that they can be counted on one hand. Without the moths to eat, pygmy possums are starving to death.[7]

We are never on our own. Our relationships always web us into the world. Yet because insects are not charismatic, our indifference – and our incapacity to care for something so different to ourselves – is causing their deaths.

It takes effort to care, because care is labour. Care is looking at a golden orb-weaver spider, feeling weird and cross-eyed, and agreeing to like it anyway. It is lobbying politicians to change the intensive agriculture that is a large part of insect populations' demise. It is avoiding the use of chemicals in your garden, even though a caterpillar has chewed through your monstera plant. Care is my partner's respect for my happiness; it is my flights to Brisbane; it is fetching coffee for one another in the morning; it is reading each other's work; it is my patience that we will eventually find an equilibrium though we live in different states. For from the work comes joy: stepping out of the taxi in front of the house, unlocking the door and calling out for him, waiting for his tread on the stair, the relief of his arms around me, like petrichor released by dry earth after rain.

*

In the year of the floods in Brisbane, in 2011, I was a few years away from meeting Bruce. I hung out my washing on the patch of lawn outside my apartment and noticed golden orbs proliferating, their webs stretching between the wires, and between the neighbour's jasmine vine and the clothesline frame. I pegged out my T-shirts, trying to avoid their webs. When the sun set, I brought the washing in, inhaling the sweet smell of my T-shirts before folding them and placing them in my washing basket.

When I looked up, I saw the spiders' webs illuminated against the stars. They looked like another layer of constellations. I did not know it then, but golden orbs build their webs to last for years.

On the Wing

After three months with my parents by the coast during the first lockdown of 2020, I was finally allowed across the border to be with Bruce again. Our house was on a busy road, one-and-a-half blocks from the Brisbane River, but during lockdown the traffic lessened.

Without the buses rushing past, I heard other sounds emerge. One still evening, during the three-day lockdown of early January in 2021, I heard the long, plaintive call of the bush stone-curlew.

'Where is the bird?' I asked Bruce.

'Probably down by the river.'

'But how can I hear it? I can't hear anything more than a metre away.'

'It's probably bouncing off the houses,' he said.

It was also a warm night, and sound travels faster at warm temperatures.

*

In the soundproofed room at the audiologists, with carpet on the floor and walls, I take out my hearing aid and the audiologist places a set of headphones over my ears. Sitting at the desk opposite, she plays a series of sounds, either rising or decreasing in pitch and loudness, from an audiometer. I press a button on a handheld device when I hear each sound. The audiologist notes the points at which I can hear onto an audiogram. This is a grid divided by hertz (the pitch at which someone can hear) and decibels (the volume). On the audiogram the circles and squares signal what the left and right ears can hear (fig. 1).

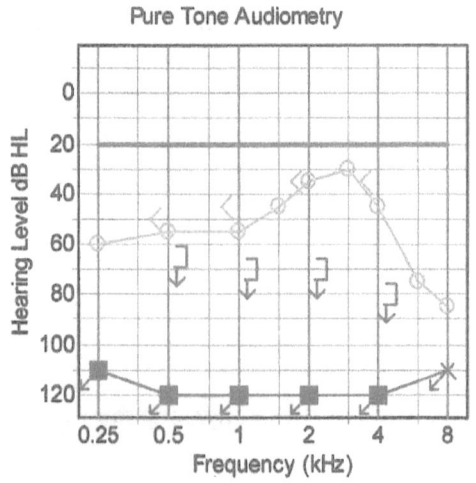

Fig. 1. Jessica's audiogram.

The line mapping my right ear's hearing looks like a wave rising and crashing. I can hear 250 hertz – the sound of a kick drum or a bass guitar, according to the app Decibel Pro – at 60 decibels, or the volume of a normal conversation. I can hear high vocals, or 500 hertz, at 65 decibels, when they are between the volume of a dishwasher and a vacuum cleaner. At 45 decibels I can hear a piccolo or soprano, which sustains pitches of 150 hertz. At 200 and 300 hertz, my hearing is closest to the average, at 37 and 30 decibels respectively. After that, for frequencies from 300 to 800 hertz, my hearing dramatically falls away.

The left ear, meanwhile, is tested by putting some noise into my right ear (known as 'masking') so that the right ear can't pick up the sounds. I have never been able to hear anything from my left ear. On the audiogram it looks like an undertow pulled over stout rocks.

*

In the late afternoon, I walked along Warperup Creek, which edges the town of Margaret River on Wadandi Noongar boodja. It was a few years after the Covid-19 lockdowns. After moving to Adelaide in Kaurna country, I continued my trips to Noongar boodja for my long-term work-in-progress, the ecobiography of Georgiana Molloy. Back in Armidale on Anaiwan country, on the east coast, my mother was dying, the struggle to pull air into her lungs wearing down the rest of her body. My muscles thrummed with the anxiety of impending loss.

To be a guest on Wadandi Noongar country is like exhaling, although I was mindful that I had not been invited there. I acknowledged the plants, animals, water and soil around me. The hovea flourished, breaths of deep purple puffing over the scrub. The creek was still, reflecting the reedy banks and tall karri trees, their trunks transmuted into gold by the lowering sun. At one point I heard the croak of frogs and was transported to my childhood, when green tree frogs clung to the verandah gauze on rainy nights. Frogs mean a healthy ecosystem, and my heart was glad.

The walking track ended before I was ready, so I peeled off through some state forest to my left and ended up near an airstrip. In the distance I noticed another track leading back into the forest, and followed it. In the quiet, I heard the grumble of an engine and, looking over my shoulder, saw a car approaching. I stepped off the road. I didn't think much of it, until the car returned and I noticed the driver and passenger were male. For all of the time that I'd walked at Wooditup (the Noongar name for Margaret River), I'd seen men running or cycling, or families with children. I had passed only one woman, white-haired and walking with a confident stride. Unnerved, I turned right, heading through the trees until I reached a tarmac road. I checked for cars, climbed over the barrier and ran across the road, into the forest on the other side. Perhaps because the sun was dropping, the place seemed eerily hushed. The monotony of the pines and the lack of an understorey was unsettling. When I saw a blaze of late-flowering wattle, my pulse settled.

*

I don't know the frequency of the black cockatoo's call, or if I can hear it because of its loud volume and distinct pitch. I can recognise its voice above all other calls in the bush and, looking around, can sometimes trace it to its source: a pair of black birds above, their wings like fans unfurled against the sky. I am constantly delighted that I can hear the sound. Humans need both ears working together to locate the source of a noise, but I only have half an ear and my eyes.

Hearing moulds what we think is important. Once, on a still, hot day, I walked in Kings Park in Boorloo/Perth, an important gathering ground for Whadjuk Noongar people. No one else was around, and the shrubs and trees on either side of the park were thick, blocking out any noise beyond. I heard, distinctly, a cracking sound, and paused. Growing up on a farm, we were always told to keep still if we saw a snake. I couldn't tell where the noise was coming from. Not being able to locate anything on the ground, I looked up and saw a black cockatoo in the fork of a gum tree. It held a nut in its claw, which it cracked with its powerful beak. I smiled, inordinately pleased for mastering something that hearing people take for granted.

On subsequent trips to Noongar boodja, I was always thrilled to hear the call of the black cockatoo. I would look up and usually see a pair flying overhead. These creatures are not only aurally striking, but also beautiful. The red-tailed cockatoo's comb, and the feathers surrounding their eyes, are dusted with yellow spots, as though a galaxy has come to rest gently on their face. When they fly, their tail feathers spread out like a red cape.

Four of the five species of black cockatoo are in decline across Australia, largely due to deforestation. They form bonded pairs for their half-century lives. The Noongar names for the species in the south-west are ngloak (Baudin's cockatoo) and ngoorlark (Carnaby's cockatoo). These species have white tails and are endangered. The karak (forest red-tailed cockatoo) is vulnerable. They roost and nest in old, large trees, and return to the same trees each time. Their memory of trees is passed down, too, for they travel along multi-generational pathways.¹ How confusing it must be for the cockatoos to fly back and find their homes removed.

*

Women's voices are, on average, an octave higher than men's, ranging from 165 to 255 hertz. This is the pitch at which I can hear sound best. I gravitate towards women because I know I will be able to hear them without straining. Many people, however, prefer to listen to men, whose vocal cords are elongated and thickened by testosterone.

Research in psychology indicates that people invest men and women with lower voices with more authority. A 1998 study, which compared twenty-eight recordings of Australian women's voices made in 1956 with another twenty-eight recordings made in 1993, found that women's voices were significantly deeper decades later – by 23 hertz. The researchers surmise that cultural factors have influenced this shift.²

*

The field of ecoacoustics examines sound produced by animals and plants.³ Bernie Krause, an American sound ecologist, has been recording soundscapes of the natural world for several decades. When he began recording in the 1970s, he could 'record for ten hours and capture one hour of usable material, good enough for an album or a film soundtrack or a museum installation'. By 2013, however, it could 'take up to one thousand hours or more to capture the same thing'. Deforestation, global heating and humans' noise pollution have affected the sound produced by healthy ecologies. Krause adds that half of his archive 'comes from habitats so radically altered that they're either silent or can no longer be heard in any of their original form'.[4]

One of Krause's sound recordings is from a forest in California's Sugarloaf Ridge State Park, which he visits regularly as he lives close by. In 2004, when the stream in the park was full, he recorded birdsong from 'dark-eyed juncos, golden-crowned and white-crowned sparrows, California towhees, acorn woodpeckers, black-headed grosbeaks, American robins, Brewer's sparrows, red-shouldered hawks, pileated woodpeckers, and wild turkeys'.[5] Between 2009 and 2015, when the California drought dried up the stream, the soundscape dwindled in its diversity and intensity.

Researchers have also discovered that the soil makes sound. Recorders and specialised microphones attached to probes in the ground pick up crackles, clicks and pops. Organisms such as earthworms make these sounds as they move through the soil. Healthy and restored soils have a higher diversity of noise than degraded soils.[6]

If ecosystems are quiet, it seems that we should pay attention to them.

*

My associating of black cockatoos with Noongar boodja was so strong that when I heard their distinctive call on Bundjalung country at Ocean Shores in New South Wales, I wasn't confident of what I was hearing. My mother had died a fortnight before after a stressful decline, and my brother, my partner and I took my father away from the endless stream of visitors to recuperate at the beach. We were in shock, and we were exhausted, particularly my father. He had been my mother's full-time carer for two years.

'I think that's a black cockatoo,' I said to him when I heard the call in the late afternoon. They were probably yellow-tailed black cockatoos, *Calyptorhynchus funereus*, which have a yellow patch on their cheek and yellow panels on their tails. Or they may have been glossy black cockatoos, *Calyptorhynchus lathami*, colloquially known as 'glossies'. They are listed as vulnerable in the region because two types of trees they rely on for food and nesting – she-oaks and hollow eucalypts – are declining. The 2019 and 2020 bushfires then decimated about 50 per cent of their remaining habitat.

The next evening we sat on New Brighton Beach, catching the last of the sun before packing up and heading back to the house. I heard the distinctive calls of the cockatoos once again and turned my head to look for them. A flock had gathered in the tall pine behind me, tearing nuts from the tree and cracking them in their beaks.

It seemed a small foothold; a place where I was held in their calls.

*

In Adelaide, I missed my partner like a plant needing sunshine. It irritated me when people assumed that, because we lived in separate states, we were going to break up. Our relationship is inviolate, but spending time together requires flying to and from Brisbane. A round trip generates 0.7 tonnes of carbon. The number of flights I made still generated less carbon than running a car for a year, and I don't own a car. I figured I also had carbon in the carbon bank because we had decided not to have children. However, in 2023, when my mother began to die, I was more often away than I was on Kaurna country. I ended the year dispirited and unsettled. All I wanted was a stable place to live, with my partner and family within reach.

*

On one of my trips to Boorloo/Perth, I had a long lunch with two friends, a writer and a botanist, in the botanist's house, a weatherboard with a big, rambling garden. It reminded me of my grandparents' place on the farm, which I often visited when I was bored during the school holidays. I would find my grandmother kneeling at the edge of the lawn, digging out weeds from a flower bed or scattering straw over the soil to keep the moisture in.

After lunch, we drank cups of tea in fine-boned china, then stood on the steps at the back of the house to look at the garden, dotted with natives. It was very dry that spring.

A few pairs of karaks, the forest red-tailed cockatoos, flew overhead. Some paused and alighted in a big old gum tree.

'There used to be thousands of them,' my botanist friend observed sadly.

We listened to the quiet afternoon. I imagined the cockatoos' wings once stitching black sails across the sky.

*

The concept of charismatic species is often used in conservation science. Jamie Lorimer, an environmental geographer, suggests that what natural historians refer to as an organism's 'jizz' – the unique properties that differentiate it from others, such as the sound of its call or song, its size, shape and speed – together with the way its ecological rhythms intersect with humans', constitutes a species' 'ecological charisma'. A footnote in Lorimer's paper indicates that the etymology of 'jizz' is contested, but a 'popular attribution' links the word to the corruption of the acronym GISS – General Impression of Size and Shape – which was borrowed from World War II aircraft spotters.[7] Weirdly, Lorimer, a professor of environmental geography at Oxford, makes no mention of the other meaning of 'jizz' – namely, semen – even though the word stems from 'jism', meaning energy and strength. To me there seems to be a correlation, with both words referring to vitality.

A focus on charismatic animals can be positive, because many people will respond to a conservation project if it involves, or is represented by, a charismatic animal (for example, the World Wildlife Fund's logo features a panda bear). Numerous keystone species – those that are integral to the survival of other species in an ecosystem, such as wolves or big cats – are charismatic animals. They regulate the animals that eat plants, and thus the plants themselves. Researchers maintain that by highlighting the appeal of these animals, entire ecosystems can be protected.

Other researchers contest this, pointing out that many endangered charismatic species are not keystone species. Rather, they argue, it is better to focus on supporting 'engineer' or 'foundation' species, such as corals, shellfish, insects, echinoderms, worms, plants and algae.[8]

*

Charisma is subjective and culturally constructed. The killer whale or orca (*Orcinus orca*), despite its fearsome name, became a famous charismatic species after the release of the film *Free Willy* (1993). In an

Australian context, koalas are considered charismatic because of their big eyes and fluffy faces (embodying an 'anthropomorphic *woolly charisma*', as Lorimer puts it). Yet it wasn't always so; until 1927 they were officially allowed to be killed for their fur, with millions of pelts exported to the United States and the United Kingdom.[9]

In my instance, the birds seem charismatic because I can detect their song with the residue of my hearing. I am also, against Australian cultural norms, drawn to women's voices rather than men's because I can hear them more clearly.

A 2019 study drawing on the experiences of thirty-one people with congenital and acquired sight impairment found that listening to birds provoked creativity and wonder. Some participants, listening to particular species, devised stories about what they were hearing – for example, arguments between crows or territorial fights between buzzards and crows. Others, hearing birdsong in a woodland in spring, described it as 'like being in a cathedral'.[10] The study's author suggests that, because of these experiences, Lorimer's definition of charisma should be expanded to include *sonic charisma*, or the charming songs of birds.

*

Driving east from Anaiwan country, the cleared paddocks give way to the tall, airy Gondwana forests near Dorrigo on Gumbaynngirr country. One summer, travelling with my parents to the coast, we wound down the windows to give the dogs some air. After a wet summer, there were more cicadas than usual. Their mating song roared into the car, shocking in its loudness. The dogs, unperturbed, sniffed the breeze.

Another time, a few years later, we opened the windows to hear the high, piping sounds of the bellbirds. Also known as bell miners, they are honeyeaters and defend their territory aggressively. On other occasions I heard the call of the whipbirds, a long, drawn-out note followed by a crack, and a few warbling notes. It wasn't until my father told me that it was a duet between a male and a female that I listened hard for the female bird's song, and I eventually detected it.

Whenever I hear these birds, now, on trips to the east coast, their calls thread me back to my family.

*

Judith Wright's difficulty with hearing is not evident in her writing, which uses rhyme and onomatopoeia, because she was able to hear well until the age of twenty-two. As otosclerosis gradually eroded her hearing, she retained a memory of sound. In a 1990 interview she observes that she was able 'to look at a bird, see that it's singing and practically hear its song, because I know the song'.[11] In her collection *Birds* (1962), she describes encountering the 'talk' of apostle birds in a poem of the same name, recounting a memory that includes 'the sound of the creek on stones', while in 'Magpies' she records the birds' voices as 'such a song / of grace and praise'. Yet these descriptions appear vague when compared to the precision of her visual detail. Wright spends more time considering the apostle birds' bodies than their talk, describing how they 'hung head-down from branches and peered. / They spread their tawny wings like fans'. Similarly, the sound of the creek seems prosaic when compared to the next few lines of Wright's memory: 'the wind-combed grass, the tree-trunks / wrinkled and grey like elephant-legs all round us'.[12]

Wright's pleasure in the visual is also apparent in 'Parrots', when she and (presumably) her husband Jack, 'shivering in the morning cold':

> . . . draw the curtains back and see
> the lovely greed of their descending,
> the lilt of flight that blurs their glories,
>
> and warm our eyes upon the lories,
> and the rainbow-parrots landing.

Wright's delight is conveyed through the contrast between the chilly morning and the warmth she derives from the spectacle. It is not sound that she finds when she opens the curtains, but a visual feast of colour and movement.

*

In 2023, as my mother's decline began to hasten, I took a writing workshop with a Gudanji and Wakaja author in Adelaide. We talked about interconnections and interdependencies between ourselves and other humans and nonhumans. I mentioned that I was writing an essay to give to my mother before she died, in which I described the persistent image of the curlew and its song.

'Do you know what the curlew means for Aboriginal people?' she asked.

I shook my head.

'It means sadness is coming.'

*

In Adelaide I live on a quiet street with few trees, so there isn't much birdsong. Sometimes, when it's raining, a pair of pigeons perch on the garage roller door to keep dry. With my hearing aid in, I can hear them cooing gently. One spring a bird sang and sang for a mate. Its tune was lyrical, but went on for so long that it started to drive me mad. I made a recording of it on my phone and played it to my science writer friend Danielle.

'That's a blackbird,' she said. A British bird.

British songbirds were introduced to Australia by colonisers who wanted to replicate the soundscapes of the homes they had left behind, to make the land seem less foreign. The colonisers complained that Australian birds didn't sound melodious. The famous ornithologist John Gould thought that the parrots screamed, the honeyeaters were monotonous and the little wattlebird was like someone vomiting.[13]

In the 1980s, molecular mapping led to the discovery that Australia was the first home of the world's songbirds and that they had radiated out to Europe and America.[14] It makes the colonisers' efforts appear a little redundant.

Eventually, spring passed and the blackbird stopped singing. The street became quiet once more.

*

My mother often seemed unemotional, but towards the end of her life she became more sentimental, and she mentioned to her friends that she identified with the willie wagtail. After her death, at her Celebration of Life at the regional art gallery (she refused to have a wake or a funeral), my brother and I stood before the microphone, reading our words about her. Behind us, a willie wagtail flew close to the glass wall and perched on its ledge.

The concept of the transmigration of souls has been attributed to the Greek philosopher Pythagoras (ca 570–ca 490 BCE). It posits that at death, the soul of a human being or an animal moves into a new body of the same, or a different, species.

My sister, tears streaming down her face, was convinced that the willie wagtail was a visitation from our mother. Another friend, who had brown thumbs, noticed on the day of my mother's death that the struggling red rose in her garden had bloomed. And yet another, who had also migrated from Aotearoa, spoke of a Maori saying that when someone died, the sky was crying. She pointed to the huge amount of rain that had fallen over the past few weeks. Although I remained uncertain about these synchronicities, what I did notice was that whenever someone spoke of my mother, they connected her with the natural world.

*

After a dinner in the Brisbane CBD celebrating our tenth anniversary, Bruce and I wandered through the Queensland University of Technology Gardens Point campus to reach the ferry. I had taken off my impractical high heels and was walking barefoot on the pavement, complaining loudly that it was quicker to go to the other ferry terminal, and that he should listen to me because I was right.

Bruce stopped in his tracks, and I stopped behind him. A bush stone-curlew stood, very still, on the steps leading to one of the colonial buildings. I was surprised by its tallness, as I'd only ever seen them at a distance.

Bruce smiled. 'They think that if they keep still, you can't see them.'

We walked past quietly.

The curlew was part of a group that bred in the nearby South Bank Parklands, which had been created from the infrastructure of Expo '88. During the day they nestled in the palms and ferns, and in the evening they moved out into the shopping precinct, eating geckos and insects attracted by the bright lights.[15]

With shrinking habitats, they have had to adapt to urban life, their calls reaching ever-increasing numbers of humans.

Unseamed

At Taalinup, where the rocks tumble down to the sea, you can see striations in the stone. This coastline was once part of the supercontinent Pangaea, which broke apart then slowly reformed as Gondwana about 750 million years ago. India slowly crushed into south-west western Australia and then, 400 million years ago, began to break away, leaving part of itself between Cape Naturaliste and Cape Leeuwin. The pressure of these ructions was so great that it caused the stone to compress into layers, a rock formation known as gneiss. It glitters in the sunlight and was so named from the old High German word *gneisto*, meaning 'spark'.

Nearly 10,000 years ago, the traditional custodians of Wadandi Noongar boodja looked out to a coastal plain covered with low shrubs. Over the generations, the sea rose and moved in, lapping at the shrubs until it covered them entirely. The saltwater people take their name from Wadan, their saltwater spirit. The Wejt Kwala (Emu Songline) marks where the Indian and Southern oceans meet on their journey from Lake Dumbleyung to Taalinup, out to where the old coastline used to be, before the oceans began to rise.[1]

Over time, the sea brought European men, and probably the occasional woman dressed as a man.[2] In 1622, a Dutch galleon named for a lioness – an animal that evolved in Africa – mapped some of the south-western coastline. The *Leeuwin* was one of nearly 5000 ships owned by the Verenigde Oostindische Compagnie, the Dutch East India Company, which became rich on slaves and fragrant powders of spice. Where most vessels made the journey from the Netherlands to Batavia in four months, the *Leeuwin* took a year, suggesting that it ventured off course and along the Western Australian coast.

Two hundred years after the Dutch ship encountered Noongar boodja, Englishman Matthew Flinders appeared on his circumnavigation of Australia. He overwrote the name of Taalinup with Cape Leeuwin.

*

On 12 January 1830, nearly three months after leaving Gosport, the Molloys reached Table Bay in the Cape of Good Hope in the *Warrior*. As the ship restocked, Georgiana nourished her body and growing baby with fresh food. She also acquired seeds: pink gladiolus, *Sutherlandia frutescens* and peach stones.

The Greater Cape Floristic Region (GCFR), which includes the Cape of Good Hope, is a biodiversity hotspot, one of five that exist in a Mediterranean biome. Hotspots house hundreds of species found nowhere else on earth, and which are also highly threatened.[3] The initial twenty-five hotspots have now expanded to thirty-six, supporting more than half the world's endemic plant species, and nearly 43 per cent of endemic bird, mammal, reptile and amphibian species. This is despite the hotspots taking up only 2.5 per cent of the earth's land surface.[4]

The GCFR region is home to 9000 plant species, 69 per cent of which are endemic. Georgiana, who learned her first lessons about plants and gardening in her family home in Cumbria, would not have been aware of the richness of the area into which she had sailed. Nor would she have known that the place to which she was headed would, in time, become another biodiversity hotspot.

*

Between the land of lions and the cape of sparkling stone lies the Indian Ocean. As the world's first highway, it continues to carry 70 per cent of the world's goods.[5] Back when the Dutch East India Company was at work, ships used to track north from the Cape of Good Hope along the African coast and through the Straits of Madagascar until they reached the Indies. In 1611 Hendrik Brouwer devised a route that, with the aid of winds known as the Roaring Forties, thrust the ships eastward from the Cape of Good Hope. However, the captains had no markers by which they could determine when to turn north, and relied on their own experience and judgement. Sometimes it wasn't enough. Knowledge about the Western Australian coastline was derived from splintered wood, smashed chests of spice, and half-drowned men dragging themselves onto the shore. The *Batavia* wrecked in 1629, *Vergulde Draeck* in 1656, *Zuytdorp* in 1712 and *Zeewijk* in 1727.

Then came the French who, under their revolutionary government, poured francs into scientific expeditions, regarding it as a public endeavour that advanced the national interest.[6] Then came the English, who stuck a pole in the sand at Albany and claimed the old, weathered rock for the British Crown.

Later, they built a lighthouse on the rippled stone. At night its light fell upon the area where the Indian and Southern oceans meet, a place of shifting, eddying currents, of warm tropical water meeting cold.

I visited the lighthouse at the end of a trek from Cape Naturaliste to Cape Leeuwin. For days, I had walked with a group across soft beaches, the Indian Ocean on one side, peppermints and coastal shrubs on the other. By the end of the walk, my feet were so sore and blistered that when the trek organisers met us at the lighthouse with glasses full of prosecco, I nearly kissed them.

*

As soon as Georgiana was well, after those first terrible days at Taalinup when she birthed and buried her first child, she started a vegetable garden, because the colonisers needed food and could not read the country around them. Their indentured servant, thirty-five-year-old Staples, dug the beds and sowed seeds from England and the Cape of Good Hope. Georgiana worked alongside him, pushing holes in her garden to plant seeds, picking out weevils from her precious hoard of wheat, and drawing nets over seedlings to keep possums and birds from trying the exotic produce. After six months, the garden was yielding daily vegetables and salads for dinner. In a letter to her friend Frances Birkett, Georgiana boasted that this was 'more than anyone can say, not even for the Governor'.[7] She grew so much food that she gave produce to her neighbours.

My mother began a garden as soon as she arrived at the farm with my father. The transition from suburban Christchurch to rural New South Wales was a shock. My father said that, to encourage my mother to meet other women in the area, he drove her to a Country Women's

Association meeting, where she gave a presentation on history. Gardening was a way for my mother to grow food for her family and to connect with a place that produced gum trees, not *pōhutukawa*. The soil was so rich and loamy that her first few cabbages were enormous. When my mother dug them up, their leaves fanned across half her body. I suspect they were so large because, not all that long before, the soil had been tended by Gamilaroi people and was not yet packed down by hard-hoofed animals.

I think about my forebears and the way they tore up Country, so tightly bound with story and family, the way that they pulled out tree after tree, clearing the land so hard that it sweated salt.

I find it difficult to reconcile this history with my mother's practices of watering her pot plants and spreading mulch on the vegetables, with my father's sowing and watching the wheat, and yet they are connected.

*

Noongar boodja is an earthly island. Scientists refer to it as the Southwest Australian Floristic Region (SWAFR). It occupies roughly 300,000 kilometres of the south-western corner of the continent. It is bordered by arid regions to the north and east, and by the sea to the south and west. As the soil has not been disrupted by geological activity such as volcanoes or earthquakes, it is one of the oldest landscapes on earth, and it harbours extraordinary endemism.[8]

The SWAFR was the first biodiversity hotspot designated in Australia (it was later joined by the forests of eastern Australia). It is currently threatened by land clearing for farming and urban expansion, fragmentation of habitats, the introduction of invasive species, and climate change.

*

My mother grew to love her garden and the farm. She went to parties with my father and then, when she was ready, had my sister when she was twenty-six. A son followed, a chubby, laughing fellow, but at eight months they lost him in an accident. I was born in the aftermath, followed quickly by my brother.

In her letters, Georgiana dwells briefly on the deaths of her daughter and son. She and my mother continued to feed, clothe and care for their families although their hearts were dark with loss.

*

Georgiana wrote at length to James Mangles about the flora she encountered. These long letters were starkly different to those she had penned to her mother and friends. They were thick with adjectives and pleasure. She also meditated on her garden. On 25 January 1838 she wrote, 'All Chinese and Cape plants thrive luxuriantly here, many annuals of England are biennial and perennial, the sweet pea and *Hibiscus Africanus* survive the winter, the latter bears very large blossoms and grows to the height of 3 and 4½ feet'.[9] Hibiscus Africanus is an old name for *Hibiscus trionum L.*, which is native to India.[10] It is a white flower, purple tingeing the edge of its petals, with a cluster of dark orange anthers in a crimson mouth.

Meanwhile, the pink gladiolus, or *Gladiolus caryophyllaceus*, grow from bulbs or corms. They are so widespread in Noongar boodja that some think they are native to Boorloo/Perth. However, they are a weed and in their enthusiasm for reproduction, particularly following fire, they have become a threat to the ecology of the Banksia woodlands and the Swan coastal plains. Back in their original home in South Africa, they are endangered.[11]

*

Georgiana loved the place where the Blackwood River meets the Indian Ocean. She described to Mangles how she would take her piano to 'the Grass plot, and play till late by moonlight, the beautiful broad waters of the Blackwood gliding by, the roar of *the Bar*, and ever and anon the wild scream of a flight of swans going over to the Fresh Water Lakes'.[12]

Breezes, thick with salt, rose from the sea and drifted through the paperbarks lining the shore, rippling their feathery bark. Behind them were shrubs of wattle, sharp with phyllodes, their blossoms honey-scented in spring. Vines wrapped around many of the shrubs, their flowers like red and purple sparks. Further back still, the sea breathed into tall stands of karri, reaching up into the airy expanse of the sky. The trees bloomed with clusters of creamy blossoms, drawing bees into their delectable orbit.

What happens on land, Wadandi custodians and elders remind us, affects what happens in the sea, 'so it is important to manage and care for Wadandi Boodja as one continuous cultural seascape'.[13] When the gullyung or *Acacia cyclops* starts to flower, the whales, mummang, start their migration. They birth their calves in Bardi country in the

Kimberley as the wattle develops seeds. As they come down past Wadandi boodja, this seed represents their large eyes. Sometimes they come close to shore, to the 'Gabbi-up places where the freshwater seeps out into the saltwater'. When they beach, they offer themselves 'back to the land where they come from'.[14]

It is a circular, self-contained movement, like the black seeds of the acacia or the round eyes of whales. The line made by the British, sailing across the waters, was linear and pointed.

*

When my mother died, I was only 20,000 words into the book on Georgiana. I tried to keep writing, but my brain could not stitch things together. I walked through a fog. When the shock wore off and I resurfaced, it was as though the earth had tilted.

*

Banksias, in bloom, stand like tall candles against the dun background of vegetation, their flower spikes fuzzy with blossoms. Their seed pods open during exposure to heat, hundreds of small lips opening their mouths and breathing spores into the air.

Their family, Proteaceae, originated in Africa 130 million years ago. Initially it was thought that the family originated in Australia and travelled to Africa, South America, New Caledonia and Asia. Recent research conducted with fossilised pollen grains, which can survive for millions of years, disputes this theory. Analysis of the grains shows that proteas began migrating into South America, then across to the

Antarctic Peninsula, to which it was then attached in the supercontinent of Gondwana. Its ancestors then diverged. One group, with soft leaves, crawled through Antarctica, then covered in forest. It reached Tasmania, then stretched up the coast to New Guinea. The other ancestor travelled along the eastern side of Antarctica into south-west Western Australia. The descendants, which include grevilleas, hakeas, macadamias and waratahs, travelled along the edges of the Nullarbor Plain to south-east Australia.[15]

All of the world's banksia live in Australia, with the exception of *Banksia dentata* (tropical banksia), which spreads through northern Australia, New Guinea and the Aru Islands in eastern Indonesia. There was also once a species in Aotearoa (*Banksia novae-zelandiae*), but it went extinct. Over 90 per cent of all banskia species occur on Noongar boodja.

Climate change, a global problem to which settler Australia contributes, is drying out the south-west. At least eighteen species of banksia are predicted to decline as the climate dries and warms in the region.[16] Much of this happened because of the people in the boats who travelled from England across the Indian Ocean to the Swan and then to Taalinup. It happened fast. In comparison to the time when the banksias began to move through the forests and the continents came asunder, it was as fast as a meteor.

*

It has occurred to me that, along with the buckling geography of my life for the past few years, the reason my ecobiography of Georgiana is taking so long to complete is because, once it is finished, the westward pattern of my life will cease. I will no longer have a reason to travel to

Wadandi Noongar boodja, to listen for the call of the black cockatoo, to watch the sweeping branches of peppermints in the sea breeze, and to look out for *Nuytsia floribunda* blazing gold against the summer sky.

As Georgiana stood on the shores of Taalinup, watching moonlight spill onto the water and listening to the purling waves, she would have longed to return to the people she loved in Scotland. Perhaps, tethered to this new world with plants, blood, family and survival, the ocean beyond was endless and impassable.

*

I close these pages near Cape Naturaliste, where I started the Cape-to-Cape trek. Georgiana, after an excursion to Cape Naturaliste and Castle Bay, was so enchanted by the latter that she asked her husband to apply to the governor to live there. She wrote enthusiastically to Mangles on 10 April 1841:

> What a view for a Breakfast room, a cottage with a circular verandah entwined in this sheltered spot with Nature's choicest flowers and fruit, the land of all others for Vines as the roots wou'd strike rapidly into the bed of this torrent. Then a well laid out garden on each slope and the eye to be raised to these beautiful Rocks; standing in the room or verandah the Summit could not be seen, consequently so much more left to the imagination, then outside again would be this elegant Cottage in the midst of luxuriant cultivation and opposite would be contrasted [with] these rocky heights.[17]

Castle Bay is now part of Meelup Regional Park, which means the trees cannot be cut down, nor the vegetation removed, for building houses. The slopes remain clustered with the hoveas, kennedias and grasstrees that Georgiana observed.

One of the reasons Georgiana's story resonates with me so strongly, and why I am here, is because my mother shared many of its elements: migration, the loss of a child, a passion for gardening and growing, and a love of reading and writing. Without my mother, I would not have found this pocket of the globe and grown to love the delicacy of its ecosystems.

Watching the azure sea darken on the horizon, and walking the creamy sand as water purls over my feet, I have finally made space to grieve, something I couldn't do amidst the pressures of work. It is just the start, and my mourning will last the rest of my life, but Georgiana and my mother taught me, through their lives and gardens, that something good can grow from that which lies beneath the earth.

Balancing

Bruce and I walked the docks in Cairns, looking for the boat that would take us to the Great Barrier Reef for the day. We argued about which direction to take until Bruce, who has better eyesight, saw the name of the boat amidst the flotilla.

I had taken a few days off after a conference at James Cook University, my first break since my mother died. Three months before, in April, I read that the reef had experienced its fifth mass bleaching event since 2016. An aerial survey revealed that 75 per cent of reefs in the marine park showed prevalent bleaching, and almost half had experienced record levels of heat stress.[1]

Despite some apprehension that we were going to see a coral graveyard, Bruce and I walked up the ramp to the boat, collected our wetsuits from a pile at the prow and found a berth. The ship was full.

After a safety briefing, the crew asked each diver to fill out a health and safety form. I noted down that I am deaf. When a crew member collected the forms I explained that, without my hearing aid, I could still hear a whistle. He nodded.

'But I don't get seasick,' I added.

He lifted an eyebrow, then moved to the next person with his clipboard and pen.

Bruce and I headed up to the deck to look around. Although the sun was warm, the wind scooping off the ocean was chilly. Bruce returned downstairs but I stayed on the bench near the railings for warmth, watching the sun silvering the water.

*

Fish balance themselves in the water via otoliths, tiny structures of calcium carbonate in fluid-filled sacs behind their eyes. Otoliths grow like rings on a tree. Scientists use them to determine a fish's age, habitat, diet, and the quality and temperature of the water in which they swim. When a fish's metabolism slows in winter, the subsequent layer of calcium carbonate is dense and opaque. In summer, when the fish's metabolism is faster, it is more translucent.

To work out the length of a fish's life, scientists expose the fish to fluorescent chemicals that mark the otoliths. When the fish dies, the otoliths are extracted and placed under a fluorescent microscope, which makes the rings glow. Scientists can then match the chemical signature of otoliths to the body of water in which the fish was born, whether in a hatchery or a natural habitat.[2]

Home is marked in the ear.

*

Back in the cabin Bruce told me that, while I was looking around on the deck, the crew member returned and explained that he was not to let me out of his sight when we were in the water. Used to doing my own thing, including packing up my life and moving interstate for work, I was affronted.

'I think I'll be fine,' I replied testily.

Later, the woman who delivered the safety demonstration returned. 'Do you need a floatie when you're swimming?'

'No, I'm a good swimmer.'

I pulled on my wetsuit, fins and goggles, my breath quickening in anticipation. Bruce stepped down the metal stairs leading from the boat to the water. He jumped and I followed. The water was choppier than I expected. Fish whirled around us: large parrotfish chasing little fish; a school of black round fish in a shoal that looked like a dark disc moving through the water; a couple of small clownfish nestled in waving anemone tentacles; a bright blue starfish.

After watching a turtle gliding beneath my fins, I surfaced. I could not see Bruce among the divers around me. I followed someone who looked like him, but it turned out their hair was light brown. A bubble of panic rose in my throat. Everyone looked the same in their black masks and snorkels. I recalled his mask had a blue rim, but I couldn't see it unless I was close to him. Finally, he recognised me and swam into view. He grabbed my hand. His palm was leathery from hours of bouldering in his spare time.

The strong tide pulled us to the edge of the coral, where it dropped away sharply to the empty sea floor. We floated above sandy patches jumbled with branches of dead white coral, like felled trees, then circled back to the coral outcrops, bright and lively with fish. Bruce hardly ever holds my hand and I found it very romantic, sailing over the coral with him.

*

The structure of our middle ear was once a gill opening in a fish. All embryos that are vertebrates have 'gill pouches'. In humans and land animals, these develop into our middle ear cavity, where the hammer, anvil and stirrup bones live. In sharks and rays, these pouches turn into a much smaller gill called a spiracle. It sits near the eyes and takes in water, enabling the fish to breathe.

In 2022, a team of European and Chinese scientists identified the first concrete evidence of a spiracular gill pouch in a 438-million-year-old fish called Shuyuidae, proving a link between gills and inner ears.[3] And, perhaps, between breathing and balancing.

*

I don't know if my otoliths were damaged by meningitis. In the dark, without vision to orientate myself, I become unbalanced. I also never get dizzy, and the room doesn't spin when I've had too much to drink.

On the journey back to Cairns, the wind became stronger and the waves larger. Tired, I snoozed for ten minutes, then pulled out my ereader. Bruce scrolled on his phone next to me. When I looked up from my novel, I realised that the cabin was almost empty. People were clustered on the deck, paper bags bulging. I detected the odour of vomit.

I went back to my book.

*

The Great Barrier Reef has become too quiet. Its muted reefs aren't attracting as many baby fish, who use the sound of shrimp snapping and damselfish chirping to find good habitats to live in. In 2021, scientists began to broadcast 'reef songs' at Ningaloo and the Great Barrier Reef, testing whether they could draw baby fish to the degraded reefs. They hypothesised that if they could lure the fish to the coral, the fish would help the coral by cleaning and gardening. By scraping and grazing, the fish create surfaces for baby coral to settle on and grow, while their faeces fertilise the coral, helping it to develop faster.[4]

*

Back at the hotel, I relayed to Bruce that I hadn't heard much in the water because of the sea rushing in and out of my ear.

'You should have. Sound travels better underwater.'

'Could you hear the parrotfish chewing the coral?'

'Yes,' he replied, 'and a clicking noise, which might have been shrimp.'

I was disappointed, as I had wanted to hear the parrot fish. Perhaps I had been too preoccupied with making sure I didn't lose Bruce among the crowd of snorkelers. Opening my laptop, I resigned myself to hearing the coralline ecosystem via the internet, the beeps, chirrups and clicking brought to me by binary code and Bluetooth. I listened to a recording of sounds in the ocean near Lady Elliot Island. It was like a fire crackling, interspersed with frog croaks. It turns out that I wasn't far off – the frying sound is made by snapping shrimp, which are 3 to 5 centimetres in length and use their pincers to create bubbles. The pop of these bubbles is powerful enough to stun or kill small fish, which the shrimp then eat. When hundreds of shrimp hunt in an area at the same time, it creates the crackling sound.

*

Judith Wright, compelled by her love for the natural world, agitated to save the Great Barrier Reef from mining in the 1950s. Hundreds of her letters, written in her capacity as president of Queensland's Wilderness Society, are in the John Oxley Library archives of the State Library of Queensland. Ever-conscious of the written word's power, Wright was not just a poet, but a literary activist. She likely wouldn't have heard the shrimp crackling either. But she was captivated by the visual appeal of the reef, writing of a rockpool, 'The water was so clear that every detail of the pool's crannies and their inhabitants was vivid, and every movement could be seen through its translucence. In the centre of the pool, as if on a stage, swayed a dancing creature of crimson and yellow, rippling all over like a wind blown shawl.'[5]

Losing one sense compels writers like Wright and myself to pay attention to what is not there. If silence is our habitat, it is one that engenders contemplation, compassion and creativity. It prompts us to seek connection, for we understand innately that to be alone is dangerous. Our lives are intimately bound up with, and depend upon, other creatures. In losing them, we lose ourselves.

Notes

Author's Note
1   Kusters, Annelies, Maartje De Meulde and Dai O'Brien. *Innovations in Deaf Studies: The Role of Deaf Scholars.* Oxford University Press, 2017; 14.

Grounded
1   Boggabri. *Explore Narrabri Region.* https://explorenarrabriregion.com.au/our-towns/boggabri.
2   Zainel, Abdulwahed, Hana Mitchell and Manish Sadarangani. 'Bacterial Meningitis in Children: Neurological Complications, Associated Risk Factors, and Prevention.' *Microorganisms* 9.3 (2021); 535. <doi.org/10.3390/microorganisms9030535>.
3   McLaughlin, Janice. 'Understanding Disabled Families: Replacing Tales of Burden and Resilience with Ties of Interdependency.' *Routledge Handbook of Disability Studies.* Second edition, Routledge, 2020; 479–91. <doi.org/10.4324/9780429430817-34>.
4   Sender, Ron, Shai Fuchs and Ron Milo. 'Revised Estimates for the Number of Human and Bacteria Cells in the Body.' *PLOS Biology* 14.8 (2016): e1002533–E1002533. <doi.org/10.1371/journal.pbio.1002533>.
5   Frank, Eyal G. 'The Economic Impacts of Ecosystem Disruptions: Costs from Substituting Biological Pest Control.' *Science (American Association for the Advancement of Science)* 385.6713 (6 September 2024): eadg0344–. <doi.org/10.1126/science.adg0344>.
6   Murphy, Fiona. *The Shape of Sound.* Text Publishing, 2021; 40.
7   Smith, Sidonie and Julia Watson. *Reading Autobiography: A Guide for Interpreting Life Narratives.* Second edition, University of Minnesota Press, 2010; 276.

We Were All Deaf During the Pandemic
1   Giggs, Rebecca. 'About the Birds this Spring.' *Fire Flood Plague: Australian Writers Respond to 2020,* edited by Sophie Cunningham, Vintage Books, 2020; 187.
2   ibid.; 188.
3   ibid.

4   Trott, Mike, Robin Driscoll and Shahina Pardhan. 'The Prevalence of Sensory Changes in Post-COVID Syndrome: A Systematic Review and Meta-Analysis.' *Frontiers in Medicine* 9 (2022): 980253. <doi.org/10.3389/fmed.2022.980253>.
5   Bratman, Gregory N., et al. 'Nature and Human Well-Being: The Olfactory Pathway.' *Science Advances* 10.20 (2024): eadn3028–, p. 2 of 14. <doi.org/10.1126/sciadv.adn3028>.
6   ibid., p. 7 of 14.
7   Trott, Driscoll and Pardhan. 'The Prevalence of Sensory Changes in Post-COVID Syndrome: A Systematic Review and Meta-Analysis.' <doi.org/10.3389/fmed.2022.980253>.
8   Kaminsky, Ilya. *Deaf Republic*. Faber & Faber, 2019; 5.
9   Ceban, Felicia, et al. 'Fatigue and Cognitive Impairment in Post-COVID-19 Syndrome: A Systematic Review and Meta-Analysis.' *Brain, Behavior, and Immunity* 101 (2022): 93–135. <doi.org/10.1016/j.bbi.2021.12.020>.
10 Murphy. *The Shape of Sound*; 51.
11 Rodgers, Jess, et al. 'Ableism in Higher Education: The Negation of Crip Temporalities within the Neoliberal Academy.' *Higher Education Research and Development* 42.6 (2023): 1482–95. <doi.org/10.1080/07294360.2022.2138277>.
12 Hocking, Jenny. *Gough Whitlam: His Time. Volume Two*. Melbourne University Publishing, 2014; 1–2.
13 ibid.; 2.

Hostile Architecture

1   Petty, James. 'The London Spikes Controversy: Homelessness, Urban Securitisation and the Question of "Hostile Architecture".' *International Journal for Crime, Justice and Social Democracy* 5.1 (2016): 68. <doi.org/10.5204/ijcjsd.v5i1.286>.
2   ibid.
3   Swain, Frank. 'Designing the Perfect Anti-Object.' *Medium* 5 December 2013, medium.com/futures-exchange/designing-the-perfect-anti-object-49a184a6667a.
4   ibid.
5   Murphy, Fiona. 'Reasonable Adjustments.' *Overland* 237 (summer 2019), overland.org.au/previous-issues/issue-237/fair-australia-prize-essay.
6   Murphy. *The Shape of Sound*; 53.
7   Rodgers, Jess, et al. 'Ableism in Higher Education: The Negation of Crip Temporalities within the Neoliberal Academy.' *Higher Education Research and Development* 42.6 (2023): 1482–95, 1483. <doi.org/10.1080/07294360.2022.2138277>.

8   Humphrys, Elizabeth, et al. '"To Prove I'm Not Incapable, I Overcompensate": Disability, Ideal Workers, the Academy.' *The Economic and Labour Relations Review* 33.4 (2022): 698–714, 710. <doi.org/10.1177/10353046221125642>.
9   ibid.; 707.
10 ibid.
11 Hurley, Amanda Kolson. 'Gallaudet University's Brilliant, Surprising Architecture for the Deaf.' *Washingtonian* 13 January 2016, washingtonian.com/2016/01/13/gallaudet-universitys-brilliant-surprising-architecture-for-the-deaf.
12 Bauman, Hansel. 'DeafSpace: An Architecture toward a More Livable and Sustainable World'. *Deaf Gain*, edited by H. Bauman and J.J. Murray, University of Minnesota Press, 2014; 375–401, 398.

Intertwining
1   Lines, William. *An All Consuming Passion: Origins, Modernity, and the Australian Life of Georgiana Molloy*. University of California Press, 1996.
2   Georgiana Molloy to James Mangles, letter books, 14 March 1840. Battye Library, Perth, MN 879, ACC 479A.
3   Shteir, Ann B. *Cultivating Women, Cultivating Science: Flora's Daughters and Botany in England, 1760–1860*. John Hopkins University Press, 1996.
4   Molloy, Georgiana. Letter to Frances Birkett, 15 April 1831. DKEN 3/28/9, Carlisle Archive Centre.
5   ibid.
6   ibid.
7   Molloy, Georgiana. Letter to Elizabeth Kennedy, 4 April 1830. DKEN 3/28/9, Carlisle Archive Centre.
8   Molloy to Birkett, 15 April 1831.
9   Molloy, Georgiana. Account of the birth and death of her first daughter, Elizabeth Mary. DKEN 3/28/9, Carlisle Archive Centre.
10 Molloy, Georgiana. Letter to Elizabeth Kennedy, (no day) November 1830. DKEN 3/28/9, Cumbria Archive Centre.
11 Molloy to Birkett, 15 April 1831.
12 Molloy to Kennedy, (no day) November 1830.
13 Molloy to Birkett, 15 April 1831.
14 Molloy. Account of the birth and death of her first daughter, Elizabeth Mary.
15 Commoner, Barry. *The Closing Circle: Nature, Man, and Technology*. Knopf, 1971.
16 James Mangles letter books, 21 March 1837. Battye Library, MN 879, ACC 479A.
17 James Mangles letter books, 25 January 1838. Battye Library, MN 879, ACC 479A.
18 Mangles letter books, 21 March 1837.

19 Mangles letter books, 25 January 1838.
20 ibid.
21 Emma Wilkins. 'Margaret Cavendish and the Royal Society.' *Notes and Records of the Royal Society of London* 68.3 (2014): 245–60. <https://doi.org/10.1098/rsnr.2014.0015>.
22 James Mangles letter books, 8 July 1840. Battye Library, MN 879, ACC 479A.
23 Mangles letter books, 25 January 1838.
24 Mangles letter books, 22 June 1840.
25 Molloy to Birkett, 15 April 1831.
26 Molloy to Birkett, 15 April 1831.
27 White, Jessica. '"Paper talk": Testimony and Forgetting in South-West Western Australia.' *Journal of the Association for the Study of Australian Literature* 2017.1: 1–13.
28 Pascoe, Bruce. *Dark Emu: Black Seeds: Agriculture or Accident?* Magabala Books, 2014.
29 Bunbury, Bill. *Invisible Country: South-West Australia: Understanding a Landscape*. UWA Publishing, 2015.
30 Birch, Tony. 'Climate Change, Recognition and Social Place-Making'. In: *Unstable Relations: Indigenous People and Environmentalism in Contemporary Australia*, UWA Publishing; 361.
31 Monastersky, Richard. 'Biodiversity: Life – a Status Report.' *Nature* 516.7530 (2014): 158–61.
32 Wynes, Seth and Kimberly A. Nicholas. 'The Climate Mitigation Gap: Education and Government Recommendations Miss the Most Effective Individual Actions.' *Environmental Research Letters* 12.7 (2017): 9.

Swallows and Summers

1 Carty, Breda. 'Deaf History Collections.' deafhistorycollections.com.au.
2 Woolf, Virginia. *A Room of One's Own*. Bloomsbury Classics, 1993; 123.
3 Bryant, Katerina. 'Historical Figures, Archives and Australian Disability Life Writing: Reading Jessica White's *Hearing Maud* and Writing *Hysteria*.' *Australian Literary Studies* 37.1 (2022): 5. <doi.org/10.20314/als.867e51f1b7>.
4 Rusden, Heather. 'On Being Deaf.' Interview with Judith Wright, 27 June 1990, TRC 2599, National Library of Australia.
5 Kate Rigby. 'Writing in the Anthropocene: Idle Chatter or Ecoprophetic Witness?' *Australian Humanities Review* 47 (2009): 173–87, 177.
6 Lawson, Henry. 'A Fragment of Autobiography.' *Henry Lawson: Autobiographical and Other Writings*, edited by Colin Roderick, Angus & Robertson, 1972; 185.
7 Wright, Judith. *Judith Wright: Selected Writings*, edited by Georgina Arnott, Black Inc., 2022; 71.

8   Tink, Amanda and Jessica White. 'Henry Lawson and Judith Wright Were Deaf – But They're Rarely Acknowledged as Disabled Writers. Why Does That Matter?' *The Conversation* 3 July 2023, theconversation.com/henry-lawson-and-judith-wright-were-deaf-but-theyre-rarely-acknowledged-as-disabled-writers-why-does-that-matter-208365.
9   McDonald, Donna. *The Art of Being Deaf: a Memoir.* Gallaudet University Press, 2014.
10 Wyndham, Susan. 'Ace Thriller Trapped in a Silent World.' *The Sydney Morning Herald* 25 September 2002, smh.com.au/national/ace-thriller-writer-trapped-in-a-silent-world-20020925-gdfnws.html.
11 ibid.
12 AusStage. 'The Cat Lady of Bexley.' ausstage.edu.au/pages/event/70056.
13 Carlon, Patricia. *The Whispering Wall.* Wakefield Press, 1992; 2.
14 Murphy. *The Shape of Sound*; 40.
15 ibid.; 41.
16 ibid.; 30.
17 ibid.; 32.
18 ibid.; 33.
19 McDonald, Donna. *The Art of Being Deaf: A Memoir.* Gallaudet University, 2014.

The Breath Goes Now
1   Hay, Ashley. 'The Forest at the Edge of Time.' *Australian Book Review* 375 (2015), australianbookreview.com.au/abr-online/archive/2015/october-2015-no-375/161-october-2015-no-375/2724-ashley-hay.
2   Reid, Georgina. 'Seven Billion Burnt Trees.' *Wonderground* 13 February 2020, wonderground.press/botanica/seven-billion-burnt-trees/. See also Stuart J. Khan. 'Ecological Consequences of Australian "Black Summer" (2019–20) Fires: A Synthesis of Australian Commonwealth Government Report Findings.' *Integrated Environmental Assessment and Management* 17.6 (2021): 1136–40. <doi.org/10.1002/ieam.4469>.
3   Cavanagh, Vanessa. 'Friday Essay: This Grandmother Tree Connects Me to Country. I Cried When I Saw Her Burned.' *The Conversation* 24 January 2020, theconversation.com/friday-essay-this-grandmother-tree-connects-me-to-country-i-cried-when-i-saw-her-burned-129782.
4   Bradley, James. 'An Ocean and an Instant.' *Sydney Review of Books*, 21 August 2018, sydneyreviewofbooks.com/essays/an-ocean-and-an-instant.

Safety Jumps
1   Deakin, Roger. *Waterlog: A Swimmer's Journey Through Britain.* Vintage, 2000.
2   Lee, Jessica. *Turning: A Swimming Memoir.* Virago, 2017.

3 Powles, Nina Mingya. *Small Bodies of Water*. Canongate Books, 2021.
4 Horrocks, Ingrid. *Where We Swim*. UQP, 2021.
5 Deakin, Roger. *Waterlog: A Swimmer's Journey Through Britain*. Vintage, 2000; 1.
6 Bailey, Cindy-Lu. 'Cindy-Lu Fitzpatrick (Bailey) OAM – Signpost Interview (Deaf Australia)', 2014, youtube.com/watch?v=G6xkFxN1UXg.
7 Shapton, Leanne. *Swimming Studies*. Blue Rider Press, 2012; 258.

Quintessence
1 Kafka, Franz. *The Complete Stories*, edited by Nahum N. Glatzer, Schocken Books, 1971.
2 Shaw, Matthew. 'Golden Orb-Weavers: Fact Sheet.' Queensland Museum, 2011, spiders.com.au/fact-sheet-golden-orb-weavers.pdf.
3 Kerr, Genevieve G. et al. 'Mechanical Properties of Silk of the Australian Golden Orb Weavers *Nephila pilipes* and *Nephila plumipes*.' *Biology Open* 7 (2018). <doi.org/10.1242/bio.029249>.
4 Victoria and Albert Museum. 'How Was It Made? Golden Spider Silk.' YouTube, 29 July 2019, youtube.com/watch?v=Fv1qq6ypiTk.
5 Victoria and Albert Museum. 'Simon Peers and Nicholas Godley Discuss Golden Spider Silk.' YouTube, 31 January 2012, youtube.com/watch?v=-cx2YhqIP_M.
6 Hallmann, Caspar A. et al. 'More than 75 Percent Decline over 27 Years in Total Flying Insect Biomass in Protected Areas.' *PlOS One* 12.10 (2017): e0185809–e0185809. <doi.org/10.1371/journal.pone.0185809>.
7 Sadler, Harry. '"A 99.5% Decline": What Caused Australia's Bogong Moth Catastrophe?' *The Guardian* 18 December 2021, theguardian.com/environment/2021/dec/18/a-995-decline-what-caused-australias-bogong-moth-catastrophe.

On the Wing
1 Nannup, Noel et al. *Forests Atlas: A Field Guide to the Forests of South-west Australia*. WA Forest Alliance, 2023.
2 Pemberton, Cecilia, Paul McCormack and Alison Russell. 'Have Women's Voices Lowered across Time? A Cross Sectional Study of Australian Women's Voices.' *Journal of Voice* 12.2 (1998): 208–13. <doi.org/10.1016/S0892-1997(98)80040-4>.
3 Sueur, Jérôme and Almo Farina. 'Ecoacoustics: The Ecological Investigation and Interpretation of Environmental Sound.' *Biosemiotics* 8.3 (2015): 493–502. <doi.org/10.1007/s12304-015-9248-x>.
4 Krause, Bernie. 'The Voice of the Natural World.' *TED* June 2013, ted.com/talks/bernie_krause_the_voice_of_the_natural_world/transcript.

5   Tonino, Leathe. 'You Can Actually Hear the Climate Changing.' *Outside* 7 December 2013, outsideonline.com/outdoor-adventure/environment/you-can-actually-hear-climate-changing.
6   Robinson, Jake M. and Martin Breed. 'Crackles, Clicks and Pops – Now We Can Monitor the "Heartbeat" of Soil.' *The Conversation* 16 August 2024, theconversation.com/crackles-clicks-and-pops-now-we-can-monitor-the-heartbeat-of-soil-235865.
7   Lorimer, Jamie. 'Nonhuman Charisma.' *Society and Space* 25.5 (2007): 911–32. <https://doi.org/10.1068/d71j>.
8   Ducarme, Frédéric, Gloria Luque and Franck Courchamp. 'What Are "Charismatic Species" for Conservation Biologists?' *BioSciences Master Reviews* 1 (2013): 1–8.
9   Clode, Danielle. *Koala: A Life in Trees*. Black Inc., 2023; 216–19.
10 Bell, Sarah L. 'Nurturing Sociality with Birdlife in the Context of Life with Sight Impairment: A Role for Nonhuman Charisma.' *Social and Cultural Geography* 22.7 (2021): 917–35. <doi.org/10.1080/14649365.2019.1667018>.
11 Rusden, Heather. 'On Being Deaf.' Interview with Judith Wright, 27 June 1990, National Library of Australia.
12 Wright, Judith. *Birds*. Angus and Robertson, 1962; 16.
13 Tim Low, *Where Song Began: Australia's Birds and How They Changed the World*. Penguin, 2017.
14 ibid.; 2, 62.
15 Maggs, Amanda and Scott O'Keeffe. 'The Queensland Bush Stone-curlew.' *Land for Wildlife South East Queensland* 9.4 (2015): 1–16. <lfwseq.org.au/queensland-bush-stone-curlew>.

Unseamed

1   Davies H.N. et al. *The Cultural Seascape of Wadandi Boodja*. Report to the National Environmental Science Program, Marine Biodiversity Hub, The University of Western Australia, 2022.
2   Clode, Danielle. *In Search of the Woman Who Sailed the World*. Picador, 2020.
3   Hopper, S.D and P. Gioia. 'Southwest Australian Floristic Region: Evolution and Conservation of a Global Hot Spot of Biodiversity.' *Annual Review of Ecology, Evolution, and Systematics* 35.1 (2004): 623–50.
4   Conservation International. 'Biodiversity Hotspots: Targeted Investments in Nature's Most Important Places.' <conservation.org/priorities/biodiversity-hotspots>.
5   'Travellers and Traders in the Indian Ocean World.' Western Australian Museum, museum.wa.gov.au/museums/maritime/travellers-and-traders-indian-ocean-world.
6   Clode, Danielle and Carol Harrison. 'Precedence and Posterity: Patterns of Publishing from French Scientific Expeditions to the Pacific (1785–1840).'

Australian Journal of French Studies 50.3 (2013): 361–79. <doi.org/10.3828/AJFS.2013.26>.
7   Molloy to Birkett, 15 April 1831.
8   Hopper and Gioia. 'Southwest Australian Floristic Region: Evolution and Conservation of a Global Hot Spot of Biodiversity.'
9   James Mangles letter books, 25 January 1838.
10 Miller, Phillip. *The Gardeners Dictionary*. Vol. 8, John and Francis Rivington, 1768; 1366.
11 'Pink Gladiolus or Wild Gladiolus.' Urban Bushland Council WA. <bushlandperth.org.au/weeds/pink-gladiolus>.
12 James Mangles letter books, 21 March 1837, 30 June 1840.
13 Davies. *The Cultural Seascape of Wadandi Boodja*; 3.
14 ibid.; 5.
15 Byron, Lamont B. et al. 'Out of Africa: Linked Continents, Overland Migration and Differential Survival Explain Abundance of Proteaceae in Australia.' *Perspectives in Plant Ecology, Evolution and Systematics* 62 (2024). <doi.org/10.1016/j.ppees.2024.125778>.
16 Yates, Colin J. et al. 'Assessing the Impacts of Climate Change and Land Transformation on *Banksia* in the South West Australian Floristic Region.' *Diversity and Distributions* 16.1 (2010): 187–201. <doi.org/10.111 1/j.1472-4642.2009.00623.x>.
17 James Mangles letter books, 10 April 1841.

Balancing

1   Australian Institute of Marine Science. 'Coral Bleaching Events.' <aims.gov.au/research-topics/environmental-issues/coral-bleaching/coral-bleaching-events>.
2   Luell, Stephen. 'The Importance of Otoliths in Fisheries Biology'. *The Habitat Section of the American Fisheries Society* 18 June 2019, habitat.fisheries.org/the-importance-of-otoliths-in-fisheries-biology.
3   Gai, Zhikun et al. 'The Evolution of the Spiracular Region from Jawless Fishes to Tetrapods.' *Frontiers in Ecology and Evolution* 10 (2022). <doi.org/10.3389/fevo.2022.887172>.
4   Australian Institute for Marine Science. 'Scientists Broadcast "Reef songs" Underwater to Replenish Reefs." 24 September 2021, <aims.gov.au/information-centre/news-and-stories/scientists-broadcast-reef-songs-underwater-replenish-reef>s.
5   Wright, Judith. *The Coral Battleground*. Spinifex Press, 2014; 187.

Acknowledgements

This book was written on and shaped by Kaurna, Noongar, Turrbal and Jagera, Gamilaroi, and Anaiwan country. I acknowledge the traditional custodians of these lands, as well as First Nations peoples' long traditions of storytelling and care for Country. I offer my respects to Elders past and present.

The idea for this collection emerged from a residency at Gough Whitlam's house supported by the Whitlam Institute and Varuna, The Writers' House. I am grateful to these organisations for this initiative as well as their ongoing support for Australian writers more generally. I am thankful to Anna Pilz who, during a workshop at the Rachel Carson Centre for Environment and Society in Munich, suggested that I transform my ideas on ecobiography into a more accessible form than the academic essay.

Thank you to Melissa Fagan, Inga Simpson, and Fiona Murphy for their feedback on drafts. Thank you also to Renee Mickleburgh for the pun 'deaf-initely', Kristal Brown for information on otoliths, and Daniella Teixeira for details on black cockatoos.

In moving to Adelaide, I have been blessed to work with Kylie Cardell and the wider life writing community. I am also grateful to my two wonderful book clubs who have made me feel at home.

I am thankful for my disability community – particularly Amanda Tink and Fiona Murphy – for their friendship and solidarity. Thank you to Maggie Nolan and the staff at AustLit, the Australian Literature database at The University of Queensland, for their investment in the Writing Disability in Australia dataset.

Some of the essays in this collection have been previously published in literary magazines, including *Griffith Review*'s 'Through the Window' series ('We Are All Deaf During the Pandemic'), *Sydney Review of Books* ('Intertwining'),

Island ('The Breath Goes Now'), *Westerly* ('Quintessence' and 'Unseamed') and *Splinter* ('Balancing'), Writing NSW (sections of 'Safety Jumps') as well as scholarly journals such as *TEXT* (sections of 'Hostile Architecture').

I am grateful to these outlets and their editors for publishing my work and for supporting Australian writers more broadly. Literary magazines are the lifeblood of Australian literature and I urge readers to support them where possible.

Thanks also to the National Library of Australia for permission to republish lines from Heather Rusden's interview with Judith Wright, and to HarperCollins for permission to quote from Judith Wright's collection *Birds*.

This work emerged in the *annus horribilis* following my mother's death. I am indebted to my patient publisher, the indomitable Terri-ann White, for shaping my writing into a beautiful book, to Rebecca Bauert for the considered editing and Becky Chilcott for the gorgeous cover. I am also grateful to Bruce, my family and my psychologist Helen for their care during this time, as well as the Dumaresq Council, City of Norwood Payneham and St Peters Council, and Brisbane City Council for maintaining the pools in which I swam. I am always grateful to the plants, animals, insects, soil, water and air that sustain me.

Thank you also to Bruce for the reference to hostile architecture, for checking the science in my essays, and for supporting my career. One day we will end up in the same place together.

About Upswell

Upswell Publishing was established in 2021 by Terri-ann White as a not-for-profit press. A perceived gap in the market for distinctive literary works in fiction, poetry and narrative non-fiction was the motivation. In her years as a bookseller, writer and then publisher, Terri-ann has maintained a watch on literary books and the way they insinuate themselves into a cultural space and are then located within our literary and cultural inheritance. She is interested in making books to last: books with the potential to still be noticed, and noted, after decades and thus be ripe to influence new literary histories.

About this typeface

Book designer Becky Chilcott chose Foundry Origin not only as a strong, carefully considered, and dependable typeface, but also to honour her late friend and mentor, type designer Freda Sack, who oversaw the project. Designed by Freda's long-standing colleague, Stuart de Rozario, much like Upswell Publishing, Foundry Origin was created out of the desire to say something new.

www.ingramcontent.com/pod-product-compliance
Lightning Source LLC
Chambersburg PA
CBHW030655230426
43665CB00011B/1110